Evaluating Organization Development
How to Ensure and Sustain the Successful Transformation

Evaluating Organization Development

How to Ensure and Sustain the Successful Transformation

Edited by
Maureen Connelly Jones
William J. Rothwell

CRC Press
Taylor & Francis Group
Boca Raton London New York

CRC Press is an imprint of the
Taylor & Francis Group, an **informa** business

A PRODUCTIVITY PRESS BOOK

CRC Press
Taylor & Francis Group
6000 Broken Sound Parkway NW, Suite 300
Boca Raton, FL 33487-2742

Printed on acid-free paper

International Standard Book Number-13: 978-1-138-19645-2 (Paperback)

Library of Congress Cataloging-in-Publication Data

Names: Rothwell, William J., 1951- editor. | Jones, Maureen, 1969- editor.
Title: Evaluating organization development : how to ensure and sustain the successful transformation / editors, William J. Rothwell and Maureen Jones.
Description: Boca Raton, FL : CRC Press, 2017.
Identifiers: LCCN 2017003182 | ISBN 9781138196452 (pbk. : alk. paper)
Subjects: LCSH: Organizational change.
Classification: LCC HD58.8 .E936 2017 | DDC 658.4//06--dc23
LC record available at https://lccn.loc.gov/2017003182

Visit the Taylor & Francis Web site at
http://www.taylorandfrancis.com

and the CRC Press Web site at
http://www.crcpress.com

To my partner and husband, Art, for his unconditional support in helping to make my dreams come true. To Connelly and Grace for being my inspiration. I hope you believe that anything is possible, because it is!

Maureen

To Marcelina V. Rothwell. You are the light of my life.

Bill

Contents

Editors

Maureen Connelly Jones, PhD, RN, is a Senior Instructor and Teaching Assistant Professor for the Master of Health Administration Programs at The Pennsylvania State University. Dr. Jones has worked in higher education since 1997, teaching in health and nursing policy and administration. Her worked in the healthcare industry for more than 25 years. Her broad expertise in the education arena in both residential and online programs, creating an online certificate program, as well as curriculum development, course creation, outcomes evaluation, curriculum mapping, and competency-based education development and implementation has involved students in undergraduate through dissertation work.

She earned her PhD from Penn State with an emphasis in Organization Development and Human Resource Management and brings an extensive and diverse healthcare experience to the students, her research, and the organizations with whom she partners. Her management roles have included program manager, hospital supervisor, practice advancement specialist, educator, and project manager. She has held clinical roles in multiple level-one emergency/trauma centers, as a flight nurse for both pediatric and adult critical-care patients, and in pre-hospital emergency medical services as a paramedic.

Dr. Jones' research explores the necessary characteristics for healthcare executives. Past research explored how healthcare Chief Executive Officers (CEOs) lead during a crisis as part of the competency development model by identifying healthcare CEO characteristics (ongoing research) by interviewing CEOs and members of their executive team. In addition to her research agenda, Dr. Jones has a passion for helping organizations create success surrounding workforce planning and has published chapters in two books: *Talent Management: A Step-by-Step Action-Oriented Guide Based on Best Practice and Career Planning* (2016, HRD Press, Amherst, MA) and

Succession Management: Developing Your Organization's Talent for Today and Tomorrow (2015, Praeger, Santa Barbara, CA).

William J. Rothwell, PhD, SPHR, SHRM-SCP, CPLP Fellow, is the President of Rothwell & Associates, Inc. and Rothwell & Associates, LLC (see www.rothwell andassociates.com). He is also a Professor-in-Charge of the Workforce Education and Development program, Department of Learning and Performance Systems, at The Pennsylvania State University, University Park campus. He has authored, coauthored, edited, or co-edited 300 books, book chapters, and articles—including more than 90 books.

Before arriving at Penn State in 1993, he had 20 years of work experience as a Training Director, HR and Organization Development in government and in business. He has also worked as a consultant for over 40 multinational corporations—including Motorola China, General Motors, Ford, and many others. In 2012, he earned the American Society for Training and Development's (ASTD's) prestigious Distinguished Contribution to Workplace Learning and Performance Award, and, in 2013, ASTD honored him by naming him as a Certified Professional in Learning and Performance (CPLP) Fellow. In 2014, he was given the Asia-Pacific International Personality Brandlaureate Award (see http://www.thebrandlaureate.com/awards/ibp _bpa.php). He was the first U.S. citizen named a Certified Training and Development Professional (CTDP) by the Canadian Society for Training and Development in 2004.

His recent books include *Organization Development in Practice* (ODNETWORK, 2016), *Mastering the Instructional Design Process*, 5th ed. (Wiley, 2016), *Effective Succession Planning*, 5th ed. (Amacom, 2015), *Practicing Organization Development*, 4th ed. (Wiley, 2015), *The Leader's Daily Role in Talent Management* (McGraw-Hill, 2015), *Beyond Training and Development*, 3rd ed. (HRD Press, 2015), *Career Planning and Succession Management*, 2nd ed. (Praeger, 2015), *Organization Development Fundamentals: Managing Strategic Change* (ATD Press, 2015), and *The Competency Toolkit*, 2 vols, 2nd ed. (HRD Press, 2015). See www.rothwellandassociates.com for a comprehensive list of publications. He can be reached by email at wjr9@psu.edu, by phone at 814-863-2581, or at 310B Keller Building, University Park, PA 16803.

Contributors

Jamal E. Al Khadhuri, RN, MSN, is a dual-title PhD candidate at The Pennsylvania State University, University Park campus. His areas of study and research interest are workforce education and development and comparative international education. He has coauthored for the *Pediatric Nursing Journal* on "Preventing Ethical Dilemmas: Understanding Islamic Health Care Practices," and for the *Oman Medical Journal* on "Nursing Documentation in Oman."

Before beginning his PhD program at Penn State in 2013, he had 12 years of work experience as a training specialists and head of continuing professional development programs at the Ministry of Health in Oman. He has also worked as a lecturer of adult health education and pharmacology in the College of Nursing and Health Sciences. Some of his current research projects and interests include work engagement in the healthcare workforce, human resource development and organization development, organizational performance improvement, and effective teams in the workplace.

Ali Alkhalaf, PhD, is a person who cares about people and has a passion for human resources development within organizations. He is the type of person who seeks to help organizations succeed. He possesses a solid background in the utilization of advanced information technology in order to facilitate organizational change. This information technology is based on a systems analysis and design platform with the goal of benefiting employees by providing online services.

Dr. Alkhalaf's research includes a project that studied employee work engagement factors in the Middle East. It also examined leadership styles and their relation to employee creativity and productivity. During his PhD candidacy at The Pennsylvania State University, he was fortunate to build upon skills in the fields of consultation, competency modeling, leadership development, data analysis, performance management, talent acquisition, and training needs assessment.

Zakiya Alsadah is from Saudi Arabia, and a doctoral candidate in the Department of Learning and Performance Systems at The Pennsylvania State University. Her focus is organization development and human resources development (OD/HRD). Her research interest is in talent development/work engagement. She earned a BS in biology from Saudi Arabia, and a certificate in English from the Intensive English Communication Program at Penn State. She has worked as a volunteer English teacher. Zakiya completed her master's in workforce education and development with a focus in communication in multicultural workplaces from Penn State. She decided to broaden her insights into the importance of an organization's human resources, which fueled the desire to pursue a PhD.

Robert Boswell, PhD, is a native of Harrisburg, Pennsylvania, where he resides. Since 2011, Dr. Boswell has been an executive director for Nasr Consultant Group, Inc., which is a behavioral consultant company with a focus on providing cost-effective, quality services. His expertise involves organizational change, leadership development, and instructional design. Dr. Boswell earned his bachelor of arts in psychology at Millersville University, a master's in training and development, and a PhD in workforce education and development at The Pennsylvania State University.

Marie Carasco-Saul, GPHR, SHRM-SCP, is a Global Professional in Human Resources (GPHR) and an expert in talent management, high-potential leader development, organization diagnosis, and conflict management. Marie advises leadership teams and individuals to strategically manage talent, navigate career decisions, and address issues with interpersonal workplace dynamics. A frequently requested task-force group member and project manager, Marie helps translate business objectives into action.

Marie has worked both in the United States and United Kingdom at three HQ locations supporting global talent management and change initiatives of the world's largest oilfield services organization with responsibilities in North America, Singapore, Malaysia, Russia, France, and the continent of Africa. She has more than 10 years of combined experience in career development, human resource management, conflict resolution, and training. She has also worked as an independent consultant for small businesses facilitating creative concepts, career development, and business planning. In recent years, her work has focused on leadership and management development, creating, revising and facilitating training programs in the areas of ethical decision making, supervision, and leading without positional authority. In 2014, she and her coauthors were awarded the prestigious Cutting Edge Award by the Academy of Human Resource Development for her research on leadership and employee engagement.

Marie is a PhD candidate in workforce education and development with an emphasis in HRD and OD at The Pennsylvania State University. Her dissertation research focus is on high-potential leader development. Among her other interests are innovation, entrepreneurship, and cross-disciplinary or cross-functional collaborations. She earned an undergraduate degree in psychology and a graduate degree in industrial-organizational psychology.

Veronica David is a human resources professional who works for The Pennsylvania State University in the Department of Labor and Employee Relations. Veronica has worked in various areas of Human Resources at The Pennsylvania State University, including recruitment, on-boarding, compensation, and classification. Veronica is currently working toward her doctorate in workforce education and development, with a focus in human resources development and organizational development.

Edwin Mouriño, PhD, is a highly motivated and experienced professional with 30+ years of leading key elements of organizational change projects. Dr. Mouriño is a United States Air Force veteran who brings extensive experience in leadership development, organizational change, executive coaching, team development, diversity, and learning and development. In addition, he brings broad industry experience. He has served as a thought leader in his areas of focus and by enabling a learning organization by integrating organizational strategy with a corporate university infrastructure. At present, he is an assistant professor at Rollins College educating business undergraduate and graduate human resources (HR) students. He is the author of *The Perfect Human Capital Storm: Workplace Challenges and Opportunities in the 21st Century (2014)* and a fiction book *Gringo-Latino: Historias/ Stories of Pursuing El Sueño Americano/American Dream (2014).* He is also the founder and president of his organization Human Capital Development: Helping Leaders Help Themselves.

Ji Won Park is a PhD candidate (ABD) in the workforce education and development program, Department of Learning and Performance Systems at The Pennsylvania State University. Prior to studying at Penn State, she worked as a HRD practitioner and an analyst at the HRD Center in a major corporation in South Korea. Her career has focused on organization development and leadership development. She earned a BA in business administration at Yonsei University and a master's degree in corporate education at Korea University in Seoul, South Korea. Her research interests include organizational change, employee engagement, and the leadership development of managers and women. She has published several books and journal articles related to Korean women's human resources and employee work engagement. You can reach her at jup268@psu.edu.

M.J. Park, PhD, earned her PhD, with an emphasis in human resource development and organization development, in the workforce education and development program at The Pennsylvania State University in December 2015. In 2011, she earned, and has since maintained, her Senior Professional in Human Resources (SPHR) certification. Annually, since 2013, Dr. Park has served as a peer reviewer for manuscripts submitted to the Association for Human Resource Development conferences in the global and cross cultural issues track.

Dr. Park's primary research areas of interest include organizational change and employee work engagement. Dr. Park is a coauthor of *Strategic Planning* in the *Human Resources Encyclopedia* Vol 2, Dr. William J. Rothwell, editor. She is currently working to complete several articles based on her dissertation findings.

For more than a decade, Dr. Park has taught at the post-secondary level in multiple institutions and platform environments. Prior to teaching, Dr. Park was an executive manager in industry and was the chief liaison for a $200 million acquisition. During that time, she also managed her family and earned both her BA in business administration and MBA at Georgia State University in Atlanta, Georgia. Since 2011, she has served as an instructor of management, marketing, and business education at Bloomsburg University of Pennsylvania. She also served as an instructor of management at Millersville University from 2014 to 2015.

Dara Sanoubane is a PhD candidate in workforce education at The Pennsylvania State University. Her research interests are in educational equity, employability, and leadership development. She earned a master of arts in teaching from Willamette University. Her career as an educator began as a math and science teacher at the Vancouver Public Schools in Washington State. She then worked with college students, as an instructor and internship coordinator at the State University of New York at Oswego. She currently works at Penn State as a counselor at the Multicultural Resource Center. She is the advisor for the Asian American Students in Action (AASIA) program, which is a peer mentoring program for Asian and Pacific Islander American students at the University Park campus, and she is also the advisor of the Maguire Scholars program at Penn State.

Maria T. Spencer, MBA, is a business consultant and team lead for entrepreneurship at the Penn State Small Business Development Center where she specializes in technology commercialization and export trade development. She has worked with hundreds of businesses and entrepreneurs on business start-up, new market and capital development, and new product and workforce development efforts.

Maria has authored or coauthored multiple publications, including *Business Model Innovation and its Impacts on Roles and Expectations: Videon Case Study; Talent Management: A Step-by-Step Action-Oriented Guide Based on Best Practices; Optimizing Talent in the Federal Workforce: Best Practices in Federal Human Resource Management;* and *Action Research for Sustainable Change* for the Encyclopedia of Human Resource Management.

Currently, Maria is a PhD candidate in the human resource and organization development track of Penn State's workforce education and development program where she studies business model innovation and change. Maria also earned an MBA and BS in psychology from Clarion University of Pennsylvania.

Chapter 1

Why Evaluate Organizational Change Efforts?

M.J. Park

Contents

1.1 Introduction

Organizational change exists as a result of dynamic environments. To achieve and sustain a competitive position in their market, organizations must consistently consider development through change. "The pressure for businesses to change is enormous and inexorable, mostly because the competition is changing, and so is the marketplace" (O'Rourke 2013, p. 169). Innovative and forward-looking organizations understand that an organization's strategy and growth is *dependent* on its development through successful change efforts.

This success requires an organization to not only identify the right problem to address but also make informed choices as to how to correct the problem. However, this is not the end of the story. From a strategic perspective, organizations must also understand how to manage and evaluate change efforts as critical control and forward-looking learning experiences. Therefore, the evaluation of a change effort must examine whether (or not)

a. The proper opportunity for development was identified
b. The set objectives were independent and clearly stipulated
c. The correct participants were chosen and their impact understood
d. The intervention type was appropriate
e. The scope, scale, and orientation of the intervention addressed the situation

Further, evaluating the benefits and outcomes of change efforts aligns with the trend of measuring human resource activities and their return on investment. Stakeholders, including an organization's decision makers, stockholders, and board of directors, are concerned with effective and cost-efficient programs and processes that align with corporate strategy and long-term goals. Whether short or long term in scope, narrow or broad in scale, or process or behavior oriented, a change effort is an activity that directly correlates to the organization's strategy and goals and, therefore, the results must be evaluated to measure its value and success.

1.2 Chapter Overview

This chapter will incorporate the following topics:

- Organization development (OD)
- OD intervention
    - Participants in a change effort and their influence
    - Organizational readiness for change
    - Intervention models
- Change effort evaluation
    - Phases of the change evaluation process
- Maximizing evaluation

Further, a brief case study dramatically illustrates the critical nature of the evaluation process. Important terms are defined at the end of the chapter. Finally, the appendices provide a multiphase stakeholder analysis tool and an activity that illustrates the importance of setting specific, measurable, and independent objectives for the change effort and the evaluation process.

1.3 Business Case for Evaluating Change

Because of market pressures, a critical responsibility of a hospital adminis-trator is to seek ways to reduce costs without reducing or affecting patient services. In addition, to ensure quality services, they are charged with moni-toring discharged patient's outcomes such as hospital re-admittance rates and postrelease emergency care rates. For that reason, one administrator decided to focus on the redesign of patient discharge education in hopes of reducing costs. This function was currently being performed by high-salary clinical specialists, but a proposal was made that this task might be trans-ferred to nurses, who are a less costly member of the hospital staff, allowing for a reduced number of specialists. Under this new protocol, nurses would receive discharge education training, ongoing support from trained staff, and standardized discharge procedures for each department to guide the process.

As this change had the potential to negatively affect patient care, it was determined that a small-scale study be used to test the potential for a larger change effort. The objectives of the study included (a) a reduction in costs related to discharge education redesign, (b) maintaining or improving discharge education quality, (c) maintaining or improving patient satisfaction with discharge education including follow-up care instructions, and (d) maintaining patient health with no increase in the need for patient re-admittance or emergency care in the first month after their discharge.

The hospital administrator determined that the efficacy of the change effort must be confirmed before implementing the change across all hospital departments; therefore, it was imperative that an evaluation of the study results was conducted. The benchmark for determining success in meeting the change effort objectives was the data obtained during the 6 months before the study.

The redesign was implemented across three departments over a 6-month period. Data for the study was gathered through questionnaires mailed to the discharged patients, phone interviews with patients, and hospital and emergency room admittance records for discharged patients under the new protocol. The questionnaires and interviews were conducted and the data were analyzed through a third party to ensure validity and reliability of the results. Items on the survey used rating scales to measure the patient's perception of discharge-related services including the quality of the discharge education and the patient's satisfaction with the discharge education, including follow-up procedures.

In the evaluation phase, the results of the study were compared with the 6 months of data obtained before the study. The data related to hospital re-admittance and emergency room care were not conclusive and a longer-term study was proposed. However, when the questionnaire data were analyzed, the outcomes were clear. While cost reduction related to payroll had been achieved, most other objectives were not met. Patient satisfaction decreased significantly in most areas. There were two areas where satisfaction increased; however, these were areas of special emphasis during training.

It was obvious to the administrator that evaluating the change effort had been enormously valuable and saved the hospital from making a mistake in redesigning these procedures to include less skilled staff. Further, the results had a direct impact on future change effort procedures in that an evaluation process would always be included.

Case Questions

1. What was the purpose of evaluating this change effort?
2. What resulted from the change effort evaluation?
3. If the change effort had not been evaluated, what might have been the long-term impact of this change effort on patients' health and level of satisfaction with their care?
4. What broader conclusions can be made from this case about the need to evaluate an organizational change effort?

1.4 Organization Development

Rothwell et al. (2010) state that organization development (OD) "provides adaptable and real-time discipline for living systems that require information sharing to govern next moves and adjustments. It is interactive, relational, participative, and engaging" (p. 15). Change in organizations has become ubiquitous because they exist in dynamic environments. An ongoing review of the internal and external conditions relative to their strategy and business environment allows an organization to determine the necessity for development through a change effort. The required intervention may be short term or long term in scope, narrow or broad in scale, process or behavior oriented, and include a number of stakeholders. Avey et al. (2008) state "organizational change initiates from a mismatch with the environment and is motivated by gaps between the organization's goals and current results" (p. 49).

Organizational change is a reaction to environmental instability and, according to Schein (2002), occurs in one of three ways: natural or evolutionary, planned or managed, and unplanned or revolutionary (p. 34). Natural and evolutionary changes occur as employees learn to do their jobs better, easier, or just differently. An example of a natural or evolutionary change is the impact on the organization's outcomes owing to the improvement in an individual's or group's work performance over time. This happens because of familiarity with work processes and coworkers. However, managers should consider a planned change effort when the business results achieved through natural change are not on target (Schein 2002). Therefore, planned and managed change acts as a stabilizer to bring the organization back into alignment with its strategic goals. Examples of planned change are process or technical improvements, including training, that increase organizational efficiency. Finally, unplanned and revolutionary change occurs when organizations face no choice but to change as a result of internal or external forces. New leadership, mergers and acquisitions, legal or regulatory changes, or competitive actions are all examples of forces that instigate revolutionary change efforts.

As a response to these factors, organizations determine what changes, if any, are needed to be successful in these conditions. If a change is required, the organization's next decisions include the type of change intervention, whether the response must be short term or long term, and those that actively participate in the change effort. The implementation of these change effort decisions allow the organization to move from its current state to its desired state.

OD also refers to an approach that a change agent may take regarding the management of the change effort. The change agent has a choice to approach a change effort as the *expert* with the power to fix the problem or as a *facilitator* who empowers the members of the organization to manage the needed change process. These two approaches describe the distinction between the change management and OD approaches to change interventions. "In OD, the power remains in the hands of the organization's members to find the solution to their problem" (Park 2014, p. 3).

1.5 OD Intervention

"An intervention is a change effort or a change process. It implies an intentional entry into an ongoing system" (Rothwell et al. 2010, p. 26). It is a deliberate action by a change agent. These interventions are described by Schein (2002) as an active and deliberate entrance into a system to provide help. So where does the change agent begin? How do they know when to enter, what problems to address, what methodology to adopt, and what results to evaluate?

■ First, the change agent must understand the organization in terms of the impact of its stakeholders and its readiness for change.
■ Second, they must determine if the needed intervention will be conducted on a small or large scale.
■ Finally, they must know the stages in the change cycle to make appropriate choices. To assist in this change effort process, there are various models of intervention available.

1.6 Participants in a Change Effort and Their Influence

The participants in a change effort may include internal and external stakeholders. Internal stakeholders are those that influence an organization directly, such as its employees, managers, owners, stockholders, and board members, whereas external stakeholders are those affected by the business, including suppliers, customer, community, and government. A change effort is generally led by one or more participants who perform the role of change agent. An organization may have an internal change agent with the requisite knowledge to implement the change effort; however, the selection of an external independent consultant may be a critical success factor because of their objectivity and specialized expertise. If a consultant is hired, their presence is influential, and they must be cognizant of the forces they bring to the change effort and their potential effects on the change process. However, the change agent represents just one of the forces critical to organizational change.

Change occurs in a system where the participants represent *driving* forces working to produce change to move to a new stable state or *resisting* forces that work to maintain the status quo (Schein 2002). If forces are working to produce change, the change agent should make use of the driving forces in the organization. However, Schein states that if organizational "forces are not acting fast enough or are acting in a direction other than what the change agent desires, the first stage… is to alter the force field, or what Lewin (1952) called 'unfreezing'" (Schein 2002, p. 35). These resisting forces highlight the importance for an organization to consider how ready it is to manage the change effort.

1.7 Intervention Models

An intervention model is the framework that may be chosen by the organization to facilitate a change effort. Schein (2002) introduced the concept of *ethics* to the choice of a model of intervention, and stated:

Models that separate the diagnostic from the intervention stage are ignoring the powerful impact that different forms of diagnosis have on the system being diagnosed. Ignoring this step in the presumed interests of getting "valid" data by minimizing the "influencing" of the data is clearly unethical and borders on unprofessional when working with human systems (p. 35).

The two most popular OD models used to support change interventions are the Action Research Model (ARM) and the Appreciative Inquiry Model (AI). These models are summarized below and vary in their applicability and approach; therefore, the choice of an appropriate intervention model depends on many factors, including the following:

- The organization
- The change effort to be managed
- The change agent's philosophy regarding managing change

1.7.1 Action Research Model

The ARM is an OD model based on the action research (AR) approach by Kurt Lewin. The strength of the ARM is its usefulness for understanding the process of a change effort and the importance of evaluating its results. According to Rothwell (2011), the phases of this model include the following:

- **Entry:** the organization recognizes the need for change and locates someone to assist them.
  - For example, in the business case presented at the beginning of this chapter, the organization recognized the need for lowering costs without affecting patient services or outcomes.
- **Start-up:** change agent enters the organization, seeks clarification of the issue and the commitment to the change.
  - For our business case, the administrator performed as an internal change agent and worked with internal personnel throughout the process.
- **Assessment and feedback:** change agent gathers information regarding the problem and then feeds it back to the active participants including decision makers and other key personnel.
  - The administrators, nurses, specialists, and other trained staff in the chapter business case provided information and were the active participants involved.
- **Action planning:** change agent works with key personnel to create an effective change effort to address the situation.
  - In the chapter case, new training programs and procedures were designed including the process to interview released patients and to review subsequent readmission and emergency room usage rates.

- **Intervention:** the implementation of the action plan.
  - The hospital in the chapter case determined that a small pilot study was needed to determine the efficacy of the proposed changes.
- **Evaluation:** the assessment of the change effort at one or more stages of the intervention.
  - For the business case, this step included comparing 6 months of prior data to the completed patient questionnaires and interviews as well as the data on patient readmission and emergency room usage after the protocol changes were implemented.
- **Adoption:** at the completion of the intervention, the change is accepted by the organization and its members.
  - In the business case, the changes were not adopted beyond the pilot study as the evaluation of the change effort demonstrated that the outcomes were not those desired by the organization.
- **Separation:** the change agent exits from the organization while reinforcing the need for continuing improvement.
  - For the chapter case, the change agent was internal and therefore there was no separation step related to this change effort.

A key aspect of a successful change effort using the ARM is proper problem identification. The change agent (internal or external) and the active participants in the organization must distinguish between the presenting problem and the root cause of the perceived problem. For example, a presenting problem that an organization believes it must solve may be a high level of turnover; however, the root cause that needs to be discovered is the underlying issue and reason for the turnover (e.g., leadership, pay, work conditions, or similar). If an organization attempts to reduce turnover (the presenting problem) without addressing the underlying issue (the root cause), the turnover problem will not be corrected (discovered during the evaluation phase). However, if the proper root cause is exposed and a change effort is successful, the turnover level would be expected to lower.

Therefore, proper problem identification requires an investment of time and personnel and occurs during the diagnosis and feedback phases in the ARM. Further, the proper identification of the problem is crucial because it is used by the organization's members in the planning phase. During the action planning step of the model, the members create objectives that drive the intervention phase of the change effort. In addition, these objectives determine what is measured during the evaluation step. The evaluation step determines if the organization's change effort has been successful.

Finally, to assist in the process, the change effort is supported by a change agent that facilitates and empowers the organization's members to correctly identify performance gaps, or other problems, and plan their own improvement intervention. According to Egan and Lancaster (2005), "a key emphasis of AR… [is] a co-research agenda whereby practitioners and organizational members work side-by-side to analyze, implement, and evaluate systems change. The outcomes… involve… the overt solving of a problem" (p. 34).

1.7.2 Appreciative Inquiry Model

The AI takes a different approach compared to the ARM. AI is about recognizing and building on an organization's strengths—what they do right—so that the organization's members can apply these positive aspects across the organization. In this approach, no organization member hears that what they are doing is wrong, and no practitioner experiences or creates conflict; therefore, the positive approach may result in increased employee commitment and engagement.

upward spiral

The AI approach to change effort appraisal is explored in more detail in a later chapter; however, a brief overview is offered here. According to Cooperrider and Whitney (1998), Appreciative Inquiry (AI) is a "methodology that can enhance the organization's capacity for ongoing adaptability…. [It] focuses on an organization's capacity for positive change through inquiry into… the body of stories, knowledge, and wisdom… that… describes the… organization… at its best" (p. 17).

On the basis of the philosophy that an organization can create what it desires, the AI model incorporates four phases to facilitate the positive examination of an organization. While the AI 5-D Model adds Define as phase 1 (Watkins & Stavros 2010, p. 171), the phases of the more commonly used AI 4-D Model are as follows:

- **Discovery:** a positive, whole system inquiry using interviews and stories to discover and disclose positive capacity (Cooperrider & Whitney 2005, pp. 25 and 37); appreciating the best of the organization
- **Dream:** interactive imagining of what might be in the organization. "Creating a clear results-oriented vision in relation to discovered potential and… questions of higher purpose" (Cooperrider & Whitney 2005, p. 16)
- **Design:** the articulation of the image of the future; determining what the ideal state might be (Cooperrider & Whitney 2005, p. 16)
- **Destiny:** whole system affirmation; empowering organization members, learning, and adjusting (Cooperrider & Whitney 2005, p. 16)

Egan and Lancaster (2005) assert that "Appreciative Inquiry (AI) has been steadily gaining recognition in scholarly and practitioner communities... as an innovative approach to organization development (OD)" (p. 29). However, they explain that AI differs philosophically from ARM as it uses no problem-solving approach. This philosophical difference has been described using the terms *deficit-based* research (ARM) as opposed to *strengths-based* research (AI) (Watkins & Stavros 2010, p. 168). As the goal of an AI Summit—an organization-wide inquiry, discovery, and strategy event—is to emphasize what is going *well* in the group or organization, it has been argued in the research that this approach reduces conflict and may improve the acceptance of change in comparison to ARM (Cooperrider & Whitney 2005; Egan & Lancaster 2005; Watkins & Stavros 2010). One example of this perspective is the AI practitioner's preference for the term *appraisal*, rather than evaluation, to illustrate the positive approach the organization uses when examining the outcomes of a change effort.

Further, AI proponents do not believe in using a logical process or sequence of events such as used in ARM. Nor do they assume organizations are stable environments in which generalizations can be applied from one situation to another. Rather, they believe that each AI communication should emerge in a fluid and customized way owing to the continuous interaction between knowledge and change (Cooperrider & Whitney 2005; Egan & Lancaster 2005). Finally, according to Watkins and Stavros (2010), practitioners are finding that because of its positive nature, "an appreciative perspective increases the power, effectiveness, and sustainability of OD interventions" (p. 158). The way an organization makes this determination is by adequately evaluating the results of a change effort.

1.8 Organizational Readiness for Change

An organization's readiness for change affects the outcome of a planned change effort and, therefore, must be considered by the change agent if they are to be successful. Further, what is learned from the change evaluation process improves an organization's readiness for future change.

The condition of organizational change readiness is multifaceted as it is relevant at the individual, group, and organizational levels. The change agent "must understand the distinction between individual and collective readiness... [as] an organization's collective readiness is constantly being influenced by the readiness of the individuals comprising it" (Armenakis et al. 1993, p. 686).

Below is a brief overview of the topics related to individual, group, and organizational change readiness and the organizational characteristics that influence its readiness, including the following:

- The influential forces in an organization
- Employee work engagement
- Organizational characteristics including organizational culture and leadership

1.9 Influential Forces in an Organization

The influential driving and resisting forces in an organization reflect the impact of individuals and groups in how prepared an organization is for change. This preparedness refers to the change readiness of the organization's members and its impact on the proposed intervention. Elgamal (2012) states that "organizational readiness refers to organizational members [*sic*] change commitment and change efficacy to implement organizational change… [where] readiness… connotes a state of being both psychologically and behaviorally prepared to take action" (p. 46). This level of preparedness on an individual and group level is influenced by several factors including the level of employee work engagement—a psychological state.

1.10 Employee Work Engagement

According to Schaufeli et al. (2002), work engagement is "a positive, fulfilling, work-related state of mind that is characterized by vigor, dedication, and absorption" (p. 74). Schaufeli et al. define each of these characteristics in the following way:

a. Vigor—high levels of energy and mental resilience while working, the willingness to invest effort in one's work, and persistence even in the face of difficulties
b. Dedication—a sense of significance, enthusiasm, inspiration, pride, and challenge
c. Absorption—being fully concentrated and deeply engrossed in one's work, whereby time passes quickly and one has difficulties… detaching oneself from work (pp. 74–75)

Park (2015) demonstrated that the level of employee work engagement has a moderate positive correlation with an organization's readiness for change. Research was conducted in manufacturing organizations using the Schaufeli et al. (2002) Utrecht Work Engagement Survey (UWES-9)—which measures an employee's vigor, dedication, and absorption—and the Patterson et al. (2005) Organizational Climate Measure (OCM)—which measures the employee's perception of organizational reflexivity and innovation and flexibility. Therefore, the study demonstrated that organizational readiness for change is significantly affected by the link between employee work engagement and organizational characteristics.

1.11 Organizational Characteristics

The OCM dimensions of reflexivity and innovation and flexibility refer to organizational characteristics influential in an organization's readiness for change. Patterson et al. (2005) defined these terms in the following ways: "flexibility—an orientation toward change…; innovation—the extent of encouragement and support for new ideas and innovative approaches…; [and] reflexivity—a concern with reviewing and reflecting upon objectives, strategies, and work processes, in order to adapt to the wider environment" (p. 386).

Therefore, it is clear that in addition to the individual and group readiness, organizational characteristics are significantly related to its readiness for change. Examples of influential organizational characteristics include the following:

- The organization's previous change experience
- The value the organization places on continuous improvement
- The organization's ability to initiate and sustain change (Ingersoll et al. 2000, Review of the Literature section, para. 8)
- The culture within the organization that affects how change is managed

1.11.1 Organizational Culture

Schein (1990) stated that the organization's culture is like its personality and character (p. 111). A relevant example of the relationship of organizational context and its influence on individuals is found within *learning organizations*, which appear to have limited resistance and a higher readiness for change (Choi & Ruona 2011; Theodore 2013). "Learning organizations are entities where people continually expand their capacities to create... results..., environments where new and expansive patterns of thinking are nurtured (Senge 1990)" (Theodore 2013, p. 65).

However, these innovative, flexible, and creative environments require a culture of leadership that inspires other stakeholders and supports readiness for change throughout the organization. "Creating change readiness means managing in a way that encourages engagement, commitment, aspiration, and adaptability" (Bevan 2011, p. 9).

In conclusion, an organization's readiness for change is affected by individuals, groups, and organizational characteristics, including a flexible and innovative management style, before and during a change effort intervention. Finally, the information learned through the evaluation of the change intervention process improves an organization's readiness for future change.

1.12 Evaluation

An evaluation is an analysis of a person, process, situation, or condition to determine its value and whether it meets a preset objective and measurable standard. However, it is important to make a distinction between an evaluation of training intervention outcomes and an evaluation of an OD change effort intervention. In both cases, an evaluation of the intervention results is determined by the work that the change agent completes for the organization. In training, the change agent is a trainer who provides learning interventions that are short term and specific to a job, and do not have an organization-wide impact. In OD, change agents are practitioners who facilitate all organization-wide interventions and learning interventions not related to a job. Unlike training programs, OD change efforts comprise long-term learning interventions that are strategic in nature and alter the performance environment for the people involved.

As the outcomes achieved by the trainer and OD practitioner are distinctly different, it directly influences the type and complexity of the evaluation process. For example, in a training situation, a performance gap on the individual or group level is identified and training to improve performance is determined as the solution. While the need for training may be in response to external forces such as competitor action, often the performance gap is an internal problem as a result of an employee or team insufficiently meeting an internally set standard. The trainer designs the training program to reduce the gap and evaluates the results achieved relative to the standard. Evaluation of this type is tangible, directly tied to performance, and more easily understood.

On the other hand, the focus of an organization-wide change effort may be much less tangible and, therefore, creates complexity for evaluation. As noted, in some instances, training may be an appropriate intervention method, but generally for strategic, organization-wide learning interventions. Further, consider a few examples of the types of OD issues that may be addressed in a change effort: interpersonal problems across groups, or the entire organization, that may result from a merger or acquisition; structural changes that must be altered owing to new technology, international expansion, or downsizing; process and cultural changes attributed to new leadership or international expansion; succession planning to address the gap in candidates for leadership; communication changes required to adapt to new technologies and customer focus; or needed problem-solving, decision-making, or conflict-resolution improvements.

There are many complexities in these types of OD change efforts as they all relate to intricate and interactive human systems. In addition to determining the organization's current state, setting objectives, and conducting the intervention, the change agent must evaluate whether the intervention was successful in attaining the desired results. Let us examine the process of evaluating a change effort on this organization-wide scale.

1.13 Evaluation of a Change Effort

The evaluation of the change effort plays a critical part in the intervention process and can occur several times throughout the intervention. The three phases that are discussed include the preintervention, intraintervention, and postintervention phases. A change effort "evaluation refers to the 'process of determining the worth or significance of an activity, policy, or program, as systematic and objective as possible, of a planned, on-going, or completed intervention' (OECD 2002, 21)" (Rist et al. 2011, p. 3).

Bunker (1978) believed that when developing an intervention, one must include critical and measurable factors of evaluation into the process (p. 404). For example, as discussed in the ARM intervention approach, based on the root cause of the problem, the organization would create a set of objectives for the change effort; however, these objectives should also be easily measurable, with the results not influenced by other factors. Therefore, if objectives are created and used appropriately, an evaluation permits the activities of an intervention to be monitored and kept on track, and is critical to determining the intervention's effectiveness.

As was shown in the chapter business case, the objectives of the hospital's pilot study were to reduce costs through implementing new training and procedures, but without affecting patient services and outcomes. The evaluation process of the change effort measured patient satisfaction with services and emergency room and readmission rates (outcomes) with 6 months of data acquired before the change effort. This evaluation process was clearly defined and measured based on the intervention objectives.

According to Rist et al. (2011), monitoring and evaluation (M&E) are at the core of results-based management encompassing the key concepts of accountability and performance. Accountability is defined as the responsibility for meeting performance expectations and the demonstration of having met the expectations, whereas "performance measurement is the ongoing M&E of the results of a program, policy, or initiative... [and] can be measured in terms of its... effectiveness, efficiency, sustainability, and impact (expected and unexpected)" (Rist et al. 2011, p. 2). Understanding the outcomes of an intervention is valuable to the organization's stakeholders for future decisions on change and calculating the return on investment of change initiatives.

Nicholas (1979) asserted that an evaluation program must be designed in a way so that learning can occur from the results. If an organization is to determine where the intervention has led, there must be a method of evaluating the positive and negative results; otherwise, a problem might be created or compounded. Therefore, a properly designed evaluation can identify not only positive change effort results but also those that an organization did not anticipate or may prove harmful such as (a) reduced employee productivity or organizational commitment and (b) increased employee job dissatisfaction, absenteeism, burnout, or turnover. Therefore, to ensure growth and knowledge, the organization must monitor and evaluate a change effort (Nicholas 1979, pp. 23–24).

An intervention evaluation serves as an informational tool and a management tool; therefore, it must be integrated into the change program from the start. Redshaw (2000) asserted that an organization must determine the method of evaluation before a change effort begins and must define what can and cannot be evaluated. As part of evaluation planning, Nicholas (1979) expressed the necessity of (a) understanding the current state of the organization and how the organization will get where they want to be, and

(b) involving people "who have the motivation, understanding, and authority to act on evaluation outcomes" (p. 25).

Finally, to evaluate effectively, the organization must recognize and monitor the internal or external factors influencing the success of the change effort, such as the size of the task, and determine when the results of the intervention might appear (Redshaw 2000, pp. 246 and 249). As this timing is unknown, a three-phase model of intervention is recommended.

1.13.1 Phases of Evaluation

Evaluating an intervention does not serve its best purpose when left to the end of a program. According to Bunker (1978), "the potential value of evaluation is realized... only when one treats it as an ongoing feedback component of the change process.... In this way, evaluation is used to generate data to help keep the program on target" (p. 404). Therefore, within a change effort, a sequence of activities may provide direction. While evaluation appears to be the last phase of the process in the ARM, this model represents a cycle, and therefore, intervention evaluation may occur at differing stages in the process.

An integrated, multiphase approach of evaluation is recommended where the change agent conducts a series of evaluations. The phases include the following:

- **Preintervention evaluation:** seek to understand the current state of the organization and what changes it hopes to achieve; use to set the objectives for the rest of the intervention
- **Intraimplementation evaluation:** check in on the progress of the intervention at appropriately selected times in order to make intermediate adjustments; reduces delayed knowledge of an ineffective or off-track change process
- **Postintervention evaluation:** conduct at the completion of the intervention; assesses the overall results of the intervention; can be at one or more periods to gauge ongoing progress and continuous improvement

1.13.1.1 Preintervention Evaluation

Interventions are improved through a preimplementation evaluation plan by gaining "clarification of problems, program objectives, ... and expected outcomes" (Nicholas 1979, p. 23). The preintervention evaluation is conducted in the ARM assessment and feedback phase of a change effort when the members of the organization identify a performance gap and recognize the need to change in order to reach a desired state. This evaluation phase aims to establish the root cause of the problem to be directly affected by an intervention rather than identify the symptoms of the problem. A variety of quantitative and qualitative methods can be used in this evaluation, including analyzing the organization's relevant archival data; conducting surveys, interviews, and focus groups; and completing a social network analysis that provides data and images reflecting the organization's communication activity.

Further, before an organization begins a change effort, it must recognize its capabilities and what changes are possible. Therefore, during this initial evaluation, the change agent must gain an understanding of the organization's resources, processes, and values, and their impact on the organization's ability to make a change (Christensen & Overdorf 2000, p. 3). In particular, it is important to establish the organization's values and the level of resources to be invested as these demonstrate upper management commitment to the change. Nicholas (1979) asserts that "most organizational change efforts call for upper management commitment and support of the methods used in the change program" (p. 28).

The size of an organization and its culture also affect the organization's change capabilities. As organizations grow, according to Christensen and Overdorf (2000), their ability to be innovative and nimble may be reduced and affect their capacity to change. Further, the change agent must learn if the organization's culture supports risk and innovation and whether employees are open or resistant to change. Size and culture may become disabilities because they may define what an organization cannot do (how they cannot change). However, if the organization's capability is in its people, addressing new problems may be easier than when the capabilities are in processes, values, and culture (Christensen & Overdorf 2000, p. 6).

Therefore, in the preimplementation evaluation phase, assessments of the *potential* tangible and intangible influences on the implementation process and the success of the change effort are recommended. The assessment of these influences can be obtained by conducting a stakeholder analysis (Peltokorpi et al. 2008). A stakeholder analysis provides the opportunity to understand a variety of influences on change effort success such as (a) organizational resources, (b) employee job satisfaction, (c) organizational readiness for change, (d) employee work engagement, and (e) resistance to change. The stakeholder analysis tool in Appendix A serves as a useful template for investigating the types of stakeholders, both internal and external to the organization, at different stages in the change effort and their influence on the change process.

This perspective is supported by Schein (2002) who stated that to assess how the stakeholders are interconnected and their potential impact on the change effort, the change agent must perform a force field analysis to determine what change forces are at work within the organization. Force field analysis is a "diagnostic technique… [used] to analyze… what [human] forces are keeping that system in its quasi-stationary equilibrium" (Schein 2002, p. 44). Once this information is known, the goal is to increase the driving forces for change and to reduce the resisting forces against change to move the organization from equilibrium and through change to reach its desired state.

The *results* obtained from the preintervention evaluation process are the basis of the intervention objectives. The purpose of setting intervention objectives includes (a) establishing the direction of the change effort activities and (b) creating the benchmark criteria for evaluation throughout the intervention implementation and at the conclusion of the change effort. "When conducting evaluation research, it is important to ascertain up front the purpose, aims, and outcomes that are anticipated as a result of the program being implemented" (Smith et al. 2005, p. 68). Therefore, the preimplementation evaluation and intervention objectives provide a framework to support the results—demonstrating that they are directly attributed to the change effort.

In summary, the preintervention evaluation phase includes the following actions:

■ Clarifying what the problem is—What is the root cause? What do we plan to change?
■ Determining what changes are possible—How do our organizational size, resources, and values affect our capability to effect a change?
■ Assessing the potential influences on the change effort—Who will be involved in this change effort? What is the level of readiness for change? What internal and external influences need to be considered?

1.13.1.2 Intraintervention Evaluation

Throughout the implementation phase of a change effort, there are valuable opportunities to determine if the intervention is on track. Cummings and

Worley (2008) recommend shorter intervals of evaluation or *feedback* when implementing the change effort. Particularly for a long-term change effort, intermittent implementation feedback permits the organization to readjust its course if the project trajectory is not providing the anticipated results. This avoids delayed knowledge of an unsuccessful or off-track intervention. This can be accomplished formally through objective measures or informally through more qualitative approaches.

Dann (1979) experienced the value of the intraimplementation evaluation process at AT&T, which provided critical lessons for improving ongoing and future change efforts. Midway through an intervention, the organization found that the change effort was off-track. Data were gathered and evaluated in several categories and while significant changes owing to the implementation had been accomplished, many new issues were identified that were affecting the effectiveness of the change effort. Specifically, it was found that most were created by "deviations from the implementation plan, specified design support functions not available, people movements, and work volume increase" (Dann 1979, p. 16).

not all learn at the same pace →train
Flexibility – one size doesn't fit all

It was also found that additional training and improved procedures were needed in order to support the change effort. Another challenge was the attempt to replicate change too quickly after a pilot program that did not account for differences across the organization's divisions. Finally, Dann (1979) reported that three very significant problems were identified: the managers involved did not receive appropriate training; there was no on-site facilitation, training, or other needed processes during the implementation; and "top management commitment was not sought or obtained" (p. 16) before the process. This example is an excellent illustration of the extent of learning that the organization gains from intraintervention evaluation as AT&T had the opportunity to readjust with a minimal loss of time and resources.

In summary, the intraintervention evaluation phase includes the following actions:

- Selecting which objectives will be used for evaluation during the intervention process
- Determining how often the intervention will be evaluated
- Deciding what actions will be taken if the intervention is off-track or ineffective

1.13.1.3 Postintervention Evaluation

Results-based management, and its concepts of monitoring, evaluation, account-ability, and performance, closely aligns with the postintervention evaluation. Cummings and Worley (2008) consider evaluation feedback to be an outcome-based assessment of the success of the intervention. As discussed, measurable intervention objectives are created before intervention and then used in the evaluation phase to determine the effectiveness of the change effort.

From an organizational perspective, there are several excellent reasons to conduct this evaluation including measurements of (a) improvement, (b) accountability, and (c) intangible results. For example, measurements of *improvement* may answer several questions:

- How effective was the intervention—did it meet the objectives?
- Is the change effort sustainable (may require annual/semiannual evaluations)?
- What are the unexpected impacts of the intervention short term? Long term?

Smith et al. (2005) experienced the value of postintervention evalua-tion when researching changes in care delivery for patients. On the basis of their research, the authors stated the following regarding evaluating the results of the change effort: "without measurement, the capacity to achieve administrative and clinical outcomes remains an intuitive undertaking…. In the organizational setting, all relevant metrics must be used to determine the efficiency, effectiveness, and impact of change" (Smith et al. 2005, p. 67). Therefore, in practice, an organization requires this evaluation to provide the qualitative or quantitative data that demonstrate results, provide assurance, and support the benefits of the change initiative.

Next, it is important to look further than performance measures during the evaluation process and, therefore, data related to *accountability* deter-mine how well the various stakeholders such as participants and consultants have met their obligations. This includes the efficiencies of the intervention process related to time, money, and personnel costs. Further, as account-ability is fundamental to an organization's strategic planning process and its subsequent evaluation, most organizations have familiarity with the evalua-tion concept and the controls in place to accomplish it. For that reason, if an organization is to conduct any evaluation, it generally chooses the postintervention evaluation.

Another significant area of interest when evaluating a change effort is seeking to understand the *intangible results* of the intervention such as improved attitudes of participants; increased levels of commitment, engagement, and readiness for change; enhanced collaboration within groups and across the organization; or other applicable qualitative data that add richness to the numerical, objective data gathered and analyzed. Offering insight into the evaluation of the intangible outcome of attitudes and collaboration, Smith et al. (2005) stated they found their intervention had altered "patient perceptions of hospital quality [and] nurses and other health professionals formed an academic-service partnership" (p. 68). Further, based on his review of the literature, Kim (2014) highlighted the major influences of an engaged employee including the performance of the individual and organization, and the employee's self-efficacy, turnover intention, mental health, job satisfaction, absenteeism, employee creativity, proactive behavior, organizational commitment, and organizational citizenship behavior (OCB) (pp. 8–9).

Finally, two additional organizational goals demonstrate the value of postintervention evaluations: (a) ensuring the intervention's success *before* its replication at other organizational sites and (b) determining the strategic impact of the intervention on future change efforts. The evaluation stage of any process is important because this valuable information becomes a resource to improve future planning activities. However, evaluating a long-term, organization-wide change effort should be considered *strategic* as it provides a *unique learning opportunity* on how to better manage organizational change in the future.

In summary, the postintervention evaluation phase includes the following actions:

■ Assessing the results of the change effort based on the intervention objectives
■ Evaluating success from multiple measurement perspectives including improvements, accountability, and intangible results
■ Determining how the effectiveness of the intervention is applicable to broader or future change efforts

In conclusion, intervention evaluations are critical through each stage of the change effort process as this learning affects the organization's assessment and feedback practices, objective setting, intervention implementation, intraimplementation monitoring for evaluation/feedback, and, finally, the postintervention process for future interventions. Nicholas (1979) states that "evaluation in organizational change efforts serves the primary purpose of providing assessment of outcomes as a basis for further program planning and refinement" (p. 27).

1.14 Maximizing Change Evaluation

Finally, it is important to address potential issues that may be encountered during an evaluation that may negatively influence the success of the process. The most well-intentioned change agent and intervention may become ineffective if these issues are not considered and addressed at the earliest stage of the process. The issues to be briefly discussed in this section include the following:

- Internal validity
- Evaluation design
- Situational factors
- Time effects

1.14.1 *Internal Validity*

A central concept in evaluating a change effort is the assumption of causality. The organization seeks to determine if an intervention succeeded and, therefore, *caused* the desired changes in the criteria measured. This causal relationship is internal validity. Trochim (2006) found that to "assess the effects of... interventions, internal validity is perhaps the primary consideration... whether observed changes can be attributed to your... intervention (i.e., the cause) and not to other possible causes (sometimes described as 'alternative explanations')" (para. 1). The inability to rule out these alternative explanations eliminates the opportunity to determine the *sole* impact of the intervention (Woodman 2014, p. 41).

Internal validity is jeopardized when *nonindependent* criteria are used for evaluation—those criteria for which an alternative explanation other than the intervention can explain the results (Bunker 1978, pp. 405–406). For example, if an organization considers using employee turnover intention as a criterion for evaluating an intervention, can it be assumed this is an independent criterion? Turnover intention may, in fact, be deemed non-independent if the economy is in a downturn and employees recognize that this is causing hiring to decline. Under these conditions, it is reasonable to conclude that a person does not plan to leave an organization because of the economy rather than the intervention.

This attention to internal validity is supported by Armenakis and Feild (1975) who stated that evaluators must use criteria "minimally influenced by external environmental changes" (p. 39). Therefore, to avoid incorrect conclusions, a researcher must evaluate the results of an intervention to identify and compensate for correlations that might be mistaken for causation. This concern for potentially erroneous conclusions, stemming from nonindependent criteria, must instigate a thorough examination of criteria, objectives, and results. However, Nicholas (1979) emphasized that one should only consider reasonable and *plausible* alternative explanations rather than *all* alternative explanations when considering criteria for evaluation.

In practice, internally valid criteria for success and evaluation are those that relate directly to the desired change in the organization and must be developed for each specific intervention. In other words, an intervention's objectives must be created so that they can measure that the results of the intervention are due to the actions taken within the intervention rather than extraneous factors. Therefore, it is important to establish *independent* criteria for evaluating the results of an intervention—criteria that have a direct causal relationship to the actions taken during the intervention. As a result of the preintervention evaluation, in the assessment and feedback phase, independent criteria are developed and used to establish the intervention objectives. The activity in Appendix B is a useful tool that demonstrates the complexity of creating well-defined and independent criteria.

1.14.2 Evaluation Design

The evaluation instrument and the influence of the evaluation process potentially affect internal validity. Bunker (1978) states that if the instrument is not valid for evaluation, or the evaluation process contaminates the measurement owing to poor experimental design, the internal validity of the evaluation results are threatened (p. 406). As a practical method to avoid this problem, Bunker recommended the use of pretesting and control groups.

This recommendation is supported by Woodman (2014) who stated that to meet the criteria of *true experimental design*, "research design and procedures must allow (a) control of at least one independent variable…, (b) the creation of a control group, and (c) the ability to randomly assign individuals, groups/teams, or organizations into the treatment versus the control group" (pp. 43–44). Seeking expert advice related to experimental design decisions is recommended as additional considerations are incorporated in each part of the process.

1.14.3 Situational Factors

The concern regarding the evaluation tool is also supported by Henderson and McAdams (1998) who cited Rothwell (1996): "change… evaluation 'has traditionally had a lack of regard for situational factors'" (p. S116). The authors concurred that traditional models have been too rigid in the view that there is one acceptable way to evaluate change. Henderson and McAdams believed that including situational factors in the evaluation process avoided this rigid methodology.

As a practical matter, situational factors that evaluators should consider using to strengthen evaluation models include the following:

- Subjective self-assessment
- The perception of the change on stakeholders
- The impact of individual behavior
- Influences such as culture and ideology (Henderson & McAdams 1998, p. S117)

Examples of the measures to ascertain the stakeholders' perceptions of the change effort included observations and informal interviews via conversations and meetings. Henderson and McAdams (1998) also found that qualitative measures supported acquired quantitative data. Their results demonstrated that this combined "framework provides the basis of a more rounded holistic approach to the evaluation of a change program… [and] for evaluating business improvement by situational analysis, people analysis, organizational change analysis, and cross-functional effectiveness analysis using qualitative feedback data" (Henderson & McAdams 1998, p. S119).

1.14.4 Time Effects

One final consideration in maximizing change evaluation is the potential time dimension affecting the perception of the success or failure of a change effort at the postintervention evaluation stage. According to Nicholas (1979), organizations often fail to understand that some effects of a change intervention may not be immediate. There are cases when the results of a change effort may only be observed through longitudinal studies. Nicholas states that the organization benefits from creating a "logical temporal sequence of when we can expect to meet our objectives" (p. 31).

Therefore, as a practical matter, when designing and conducting an evaluation process, what can be measured and defined as intervention results may be dependent on the timing of the evaluation(s). The change agent(s) must determine if well-defined objectives require the inclusion of one or more specific timeframes in which results should be expected. In this way, the organization can maximize its evaluation process and the effectiveness of the change effort is appropriately measured.

1.15 Chapter Summary

From a strategic perspective, the importance of evaluating the results of an organizational development change effort cannot be overstressed. OD change efforts are long-term, organization-wide interventions that have a direct and strategic impact on the organization, including the environment in which the individuals and groups within it work. The change agent, whether internal or external, must have the essential expertise to facilitate the change effort with an approach that fits the organization and its culture, including the ability to determine its readiness for change. Further, understanding the key elements of facilitating, assessing, designing, managing, and evaluating the change effort may be the line between the intervention's success and failure.

Anticipation regarding when change effort results will occur affects the expectations and perceptions of its success. Change evaluation provides key learning at each stage of the process from the preintervention through postintervention phases. The knowledge obtained through the evaluation process is valuable as it may identify the positive results sought and those that an organization did not anticipate, including those that may prove harmful to the organization and its stakeholders.

In the preintervention evaluation, using assessment and feedback, the change agent must learn the influence of internal and external stakeholders on the process as they directly affect the success of the intervention. This evaluation phase allows the change agent to understand the root cause of an identified problem and facilitate the stakeholders in developing the specific and measurable change objectives using independent criteria to ensure internal validity. The intraintervention evaluation phase saves the organization time and resources because the intermediate monitoring and control of the intervention allows for adjustments and avoids a costly delay in learning of an ineffective or off-track process. In the postintervention evaluation, organization-wide results are gathered and analyzed. These results determine the overall effectiveness of the intervention and provide strategic information to the decision makers related to the value of this and future change investments.

To maximize the evaluation process, the change agent must consider the effect on internal validity by the experimental design and evaluation tools. Further, identifying and measuring intangible results and situational factors complement data obtained through quantitative methods and provide rich insight into the change process, achieving a holistic approach. As improvements may be ongoing after the intervention is completed, the organization can choose to evaluate the change effort over one or more periods.

This chapter introduced organizational change evaluation, its importance to a successful intervention, and the components and considerations related to the evaluation process. Many of the topics initiated in this chapter are explored in depth throughout the rest of this book, including (a) aligning evaluation to organizational strategy, (b) planning the evaluation of interventions, (c) identifying key stakeholders, (d) determining evaluators and evaluation criteria, (e) evaluation data collection methods, and (f) appraising organizational change—an AI approach.

1.16 Key Definitions

Change agent: "A change agent is a person who attempts to change some aspect of an organization" (Rothwell et al. 2010, p. 24).

Change effort evaluation: A systematic method of determining the value of an organization development intervention.

Change intervention: "An intervention is a change effort or a change process. It implies an intentional entry into an ongoing system" (Rothwell et al. 2010, p. 26).

Evaluation: An analysis of a person, process, situation, or condition to determine its value and whether it meets a preset objective standard.

Organization development (OD): "An effort (1) planned, (2) organization-wide, and (3) managed from the top, to (4) increase organization effectiveness and health through (5) planned interventions in the organization's 'processes,' using behavioral-science knowledge" (Beckhard 1969, p. 9). OD is a reaction to instability in the organization's internal or external environments (Avey et al. 2008; Schein 2002).

Organizational readiness for change: The commitment of organizational members to implementing change where "readiness… connotes a state of being both psychologically and behaviorally prepared to take action" (Elgamal 2012, p. 46).

Stakeholder: May be internal or external to an organization. Internal stakeholders have a direct impact on the organization and include employees, managers, owners, stockholders, and board members. External stakeholders indirectly affect the organization and include customers, suppliers, the community, and government.

References

Armenakis, A. A., & Feild, H. S. (1975). Evaluation of organizational change using nonindependent criterion measures. *Personnel Psychology, 28*(1), 39–44. Retrieved from http://ezaccess.libraries.psu.edu/login?url=http://search.ebscohost .com/login.aspx?direct=true&db=buh&AN=6260883&site=ehost-live

Armenakis, A. A., Harris, S. G., & Mossholder, K. W. (1993). Creating readiness for organizational change. *Human Relations, 46*(6), 681–703. doi:10.1177/0018726 79304600601

Avey, J. B., Wernsing, T. S., & Luthans, F. (2008). Can positive employees help positive organizational change? Impact of psychological capital and emotions on relevant attitudes and behaviors. *The Journal of Applied Behavioral Science, 44*(1), 48–70. doi:10.1177/0021886307311470

Beckhard, R. (1969). *Organization Development: Strategies and Models.* Reading, MA: Addison-Wesley.

Bevan, R. (2011). Keeping change on track. *The Journal for Quality and Participation, 34*(1), 4–9. Retrieved from http://search.proquest.com/docview /867280017?accountid=13158

Bunker, K. A. (1978). Evaluation as a systemic component of organizational change efforts. *Proceedings of the Human Factors Society and Ergonomics Society Annual Meeting, 22,* 404. doi:10.1177/107118137802200109

Choi, M., & Ruona, W. E. A. (2011). Individual readiness for organizational change and its implications for human resource and organization development. *Human Resource Development Review, 10*(1), 46–73. doi:10.1177/15344843103 84957

Christensen, C. M., & Overdorf, M. (2000). Meeting the challenge of disruptive change. *Harvard Business Review.* Retrieved from http://hbr.org/2000/03 /meeting-the-challenge-of-disruptive-change/ar/1

Cooperrider, D. L., & Whitney, D. (1998). The appreciative inquiry summit: Overview and applications. *Employment Relations Today, 25*(2), 17–28. doi:10 .1002/ert.3910250203

Cooperrider, D. L., & Whitney, D. K. (2005). *Appreciative Inquiry: A Positive Revolution in Change* (1st ed.). San Francisco, CA: Berrett-Koehler.

Cummings, T. G., & Worley, C. G. (2008). *Organization Development & Change* (9th ed.). Mason, OH: South Western Cengage Learning.

Dann, A. O. (1979). Evaluating and diffusing an organizational change effort. *NSPI Journal, 18*(5), 14–16. doi:10.1002/pfi.4180180510

Egan, R. M., & Lancaster, C. M. (2005). Comparing appreciative inquiry to action research: OD practitioner perspectives. *Organization Development Journal, 23*(2), 29–49. Retrieved from http://search.proquest.com/docview/197977197 ?accountid=13158

Elgamal, M. A. (2012). A proposed model of the determinants of the readiness for change in small professional sub-organizations. *GSTF Business Review (GBR), 1*(3), 45–50. doi:10.5176/2010-4804_1.3.93

Henderson, J., & McAdams, R. (1998). A more subjective approach to business improvement and organizational change evaluation. *Total Quality Management, 9*(4/5), S116–S120. Retrieved from http://search.proquest.com /docview/219797305?accountid=13158

Ingersoll, G. L., Kirsch, J. C., Merk, S. E., & Lightfoot, J. (2000). Relationship of organizational culture and readiness for change to employee commitment to the organization. *Journal of Nursing Administration, 30*(1), 11–20. doi:10 .1097/00005110-200001000-00004

Kim, W. (2014). Introduction. In W. J. Rothwell (Ed.). *Creating Engaged Employees: It's Worth the Investment* (1st ed., pp. 1–12). Alexandria, VA: ASTD Press.

Nicholas, J. M. (1979). Evaluation research in organizational change interventions: Considerations and some suggestions. *Journal of Applied Behavioral Sciences, 15*(1), 23–40. doi:10.1177/002188637901500104

O'Rourke, J. S. (2013). *Management Communication: A Case-Analysis Approach* (5th ed.). Upper Saddle River, NJ: Prentice Hall.

Park, M. J. (2014). Consulting for organizational change: The approach of a consultant in a long-term, large system change effort. BAASANA Conference. Ramapo College of New Jersey, Mahwah, NJ. 21 June 2014. Conference Presentation.

Park, M. J. (2015). The relationship of change readiness and work engagement in manufacturing organizations in south-central Pennsylvania. Unpublished doctoral dissertation. The Pennsylvania State University, State College, PA.

Patterson, M. G., West, M. A., Shackleton, V. J., Dawson, J. F., Lawthom, R., Maitlis, S., Robinson, D. L., & Wallace, A. M. (2005). Validating the organizational climate measure: Links to managerial practices, productivity and innovation. *Journal of Organizational Behavior, 26*(4), 379–408. doi:10.1002/job.312

Peltokorpi, A., Alho, A., Kujala, J., Aitamurto, J., & Parvinen, P. (2008). Stakeholder approach for evaluating organizational change projects. *International Journal of Health Care Quality Assurance, 21*(5), 418–434. doi:10.1108/09526860810890413

Redshaw, B. (2000). Evaluating organizational effectiveness. *Industrial and Commercial Training, 32*(7), 245–248. Retrieved from http://search.proquest .com/docview/214108745?accountid=13158

Rist, R. C., Boily, M.-H., & Martin, F. (2011). *Influencing Change: Building Evaluation Capacity to Strengthen Governance.* Washington, DC: World Bank Publications. Retrieved from http://pensu.eblib.com/patron/FullRecord .aspx?p=718832

Rothwell, S. (1996). Organizing chance and management learning. *Management Update,* 18, 21–32.

Rothwell, W. J. (2011). Fall OD. [PowerPoint slides]. In *WFED 572 Organization Development for Industrial Trainers* course. Course conducted fall 2011 at The Pennsylvania State University.

Rothwell, W. J., Stavros, M., & Sullivan, R. L. (2010). Organization development and change. In W. J. Rothwell, J. M. Stavros, R. L. Sullivan, & A. Sullivan (Eds.), *Practicing Organization Development: A Guide for Leading Change* (3rd ed., pp. 11–42). San Francisco, CA: Pfeiffer & Co.

Schaufeli, W. B., Salanova, M., González-romá, V., & Bakker, A. B. (2002). The measurement of engagement and burnout: A two sample confirmatory factor analytic approach. *Journal of Happiness Studies, 3*(1), 71–92. doi:10 .1023/A:1015630930326

Schein, E. H. (1990). Organizational culture. *American Psychologist, 45*(2), 109–119. doi:10.1037/0003-066X.45.2.109

Schein, E. H. (2002). Models and tools for stability and change in human systems. *Reflections, 4*(2), 34–46. doi:10.1162/152417302762251327

Senge, P. M. (1990*). The Fifth Discipline: The Art and Practice of the Learning Organization.* London: Random House.

Smith, C. E., Rebeck, S., Schaag, H., Kleinbeck, S., Moore, J. M., & Bleich, M. R. (2005). A model for evaluating systemic change. *Journal of Nursing Administration, 35*(2), 67–73. Retrieved from The Pennsylvania State University Library Online Database.

Theodore, J. (2013). Organizational development interventions in learning organizations. *International Journal of Management & Information Systems, 17*(1), 65–70. Retrieved from http://search.proquest.com/docview/1418458881?account id=13158

Trochim, W. R. (2006). Internal validity. *Research Methods Knowledge Base.* Retrieved from http://www.socialresearchmethods.net/kb/intval.php

Watkins, J. M., & Stavros, J. M. (2010). Appreciative inquiry: OD in the post-modern age. In W. J. Rothwell, J. M. Stavros, R. L. Sullivan, & A. Sullivan (Eds.), *Practicing Organization Development: A Guide for Leading Change* (3rd ed., pp. 158–181). San Francisco, CA: Pfeiffer & Co.

Woodman, R. W. (2014). The role of internal validity in evaluation research on organizational change interventions. *Journal of Applied Behavioral Science, 50*(1), 40–49. doi:10.1177/0021886313515613

Chapter 2

How Does Organizational Change Evaluation Differ from Training Evaluation?

Zakiya Alsadah, Ali Alkhalaf, and Maureen Connelly Jones

Contents

2.1 Introduction

So often when a problem arises leadership suggests a "training" event to put the issue to rest. This edict usually occurs without much research or discussion and typically those who suggested it feel it will solve each and every issue with a short 15- to 30-min re-refresher program. Those in the business of organization change know that each problem is unique and deserves some careful thought before committing to a specific intervention. Training can be very useful to correct knowledge deficits on specific products or concepts but it usually does not create big-picture disruptions in how people work or how an organization functions. Training is not organizational change and, therefore, should be evaluated differently. Both require intentional planning to identify, collect, and then assess the appropriate metrics to determine if the training or change effort was effective and met the desired goals. The focus of this chapter is to explore how change evaluation differs from training evaluation.

2.2 Chapter Overview

This chapter will cover the following areas:

- Business case
- The differences between organization change evaluation and training evaluation
- Evaluation approaches and models
- Workplace applications
- Definitions of important terms

Both organization change intervention and training intervention have their own unique requirements and specifications. For example, some situations could be better served by holistic organization change efforts while others can benefit from using training intervention. Since these interventions cost the organization money, time, and many resources, it is essential to measure to what extent these interventions will be successful (Alzahmi et al., 2013; Head & Sorensen, 2005). Therefore, urging the client to embrace the evaluation process before, during, and at completion of the change efforts is very important. Moreover, it is important for the consultant to demonstrate the differences between the evaluation of the organizational change intervention and the evaluation of the training intervention for the client. Thus, the client assures that the best intervention is chosen and the appropriate evaluation metrics are in place. Also, the client can clearly monitor progress and make adjustments along the way, avoiding delays while increasing the possibility of demonstrating measured success.

2.3 Business Case

An electric company identified significant variation in the productivity and efficiency of its workforce and was not sure of the cause or direction to take in order to improve the situation. In fact, after executive team meetings and lots of questions, the CEO realized that the team did not know much about their employee base. The organization was not a fan of paperwork, so much of the communication was verbal—passed from upper-level leadership to middle manager and then to the frontline staff, including the process for evaluating and then rewarding employee performance. Therefore, the CEO decided that the solution should be to train all of the managers on how to complete a performance evaluation. He set up a meeting with Jean, the human resources (HR) manager, and was surprised to hear that she felt training was not the best idea. The CEO pushed back, suggesting that each of them just needed to learn to do it better and the executive team would get better data. Jean was new to the company and worried that what she would say next may get her fired. She continued anyway, sharing that she felt the organization needed to look more closely at the performance management process including what attributes or performance metrics the company felt were important and worthy of reward. Additionally, she was unsure how employees were supposed to know how to meet the standards each year as they were not involved in any part of the process. After a few moments of difficult silence, the CEO then said, "Well let's set up training for that too."

She spent some time filling in the CEO on the current process: Because no formal performance management policy was in place, every supervisor simply submitted a handwritten evaluation on a sheet of paper for each employee and sent it to the HR department. Employees did not participate, nor did they review the evaluation before its submission. At this point, the HR department assigned a merit increase solely based on the supervisors' evaluation. There was no scale or evaluation criteria used for the raises; it relied on the HR manager to subjectively determine how successful the employee was over the year after reading the assessment—sometimes only a few sentences long. This process caused significant chatter among the employees and often resentment with the lack of criteria and missing metrics.

Over the next few meetings with the HR manager, the CEO came to see that training can help improve performance, but it would not affect organizational change, which is what they really needed in order to map a performance management plan. The leadership team set up a new performance management policy to take effect on January 1.

The new policy was different and grew from a series of retreats and meetings of the executive team to define the organization's values and then job descriptions and duties for each position. Now, each manager meets with each employee at the first month of the year and sets several goals to be achieved by the end of the year. Then, at the end of the year, the supervisor meets with the employee again to review progress to goals. HR then determines a raise.

Three levels of evaluation took place during this intervention effort. After each round of questions, a short survey was sent to measure employee engagement in the process, assess the success of the intervention, and diagnose any areas of improvement of the intervention plan. Feedback was provided to the executive team at each step.

Case Questions

1. How would the outcome change if this organization had chosen to provide short training on performance evaluation rather than take on an organizational change effort? How would it have affected the frontline staff—short term and long term?
2. How does organizational change facilitate long-term planning in this case?
3. What are the possible positive outcomes for the executive team and middle management when using organizational change?
4. What are the benefits to the employees when organization change is the focus?

2.4 Training versus Organization Development

Training is the process of learning the skills needed to do a particular job or activity (Cambridge University Press, 2016). Training in an organization has many benefits. It equips employees with necessary skills to perform their jobs and, when evaluated and monitored, can help employees understand what is expected—often leading to increased morale and provides a good tool for the organization to meet stated outcomes. Training also can assist new employees to orient and assimilate into their organizations, therefore increasing work engagement and reducing turnover. Moreover, training is important in the knowledge transfer from experts to other employees. Training has a specific target and should be used to introduce, improve, or re-educate employees in a certain subject. It has a beginning and an end and can be easily evaluated using a variety of metrics: pretests and posttests, demonstration, self-assessment, observation, quizzes, and other short-term measurements.

To understand the difference between organizational change evaluation and training evaluation, it is essential to further understand the difference between organization development (OD) and training. When an organization is facing a new challenge, crisis, or a need to implement change effort, the first thing that management typically asks for is training. Training is considered a short-term change as a response to a current or future need of learning new skills or developing new knowledge (Rothwell & Graber, 2010; Rothwell & Sredl, 2000). Employees may also be expected to attend a training program as an effort to change their minds, beliefs, morals, attitudes, and so on. Organizations tend to train employees to stay competitive in some areas and align the learning with organization's goals. Another use for training comes after a needs assessment is completed. Training may be indicated if it meets the above objectives and might be included as a part of an overall change effort but will not be adequate as the change effort.

There are two main models for conducting OD: the Action Research Model (entry, start-up, assessment and feedback, action planning, intervention, evaluation, adoption, and separation) and the Appreciative Inquiry model (discovery, dream, design, and destiny). Both are discussed in-depth in Chapter 1 and show the importance of evaluation on a continual basis. Here is a summary to clarify the benefits of these types of evaluation.

2.5 Action Research

Lewin developed a methodology that improved the system and conceptualized a theory in the process (Bushe, 2000). His concept, known as action research, included "interweaving of laboratory experiment, systematic research in the field, and client service" (Papanek, 1973, p. 317). Lewin believed that the motivation to change was strongly related to action. So, if people are active in decisions that affect them, they are more likely to change. Lewin's work initiated the creation of an approach to learning about groups, participation in groups, interpersonal relations, and change. This approach was developed through action research and the T-group (a group of people engage in intensive evaluation, by peers and instructors, in order to improve their skills). For Lewin, it was not enough to try to explain things; one also had to try to change them, and one had to involve others (the T-group) in that process of understanding and changing. Thus, working at changing human systems often involved variables that could not be controlled by traditional research methods in the physical sciences (Coghlan & Claus, 2005; White, 2004). The idea of action research was born when Lewin focused "on the need to bridge the gap between science and the realm of practical affairs. Science, he said, should be used to inform and educate social practice, and subsequent action then would inform science" (Cooperrider & Srivastva, 1987, p. 150).

There are three steps in Lewin's description of the process of change:

Step 1. Unfreezing: the individual or group becomes aware of a need to change.

Step 2. Changing: the situation is diagnosed and new models of behavior are explored and tested.

Step 3. Refreezing: application of new behavior is evaluated and adopted.

Action research is a cyclical process of change. The cycle begins with a series of planning actions initiated by the client and the change agent working together. The principal elements of this stage include a preliminary diagnosis, data gathering, feedback of results, and joint action planning. The second stage of action research is the action, or transformation, phase. The third stage of action research is the output phase. This stage includes actual changes in behavior (if any) resulting from corrective action steps taken after the second stage.

2.6 Appreciative Inquiry

So often a change effort can be well meaning but poorly executed, causing negative feelings in both the leadership and employee bases. Negative feelings and actions can arise if the concerns are not addressed and managed. Change can also bring about negative consequences, such as fear, stress, and anxiety (Watkins & Mohr, 2001). For example, employees might be afraid of getting fired; therefore, they might resist change. Resistance to change remains inevitable and sometimes threatens the success of change initiatives (French & Bell, 1995). However, in the OD toolbox, there exists another approach that focuses on the positive, and actively seeks employee engagement at all levels (as appropriate). Appreciative Inquiry (AI) starts by recognizing an organization's strengths as resources for change (Sekerka et al., 2006). "Research has shown that building on people's strengths can produce greater results than spending time correcting their weaknesses" (Buckingham & Clifton, 2001; Clifton & Harter, 2003; Rath & Conchie, 2009). Moreover, AI reduces the negative feelings associated with change interventions (Sekerka et al., 2006). AI creates "a positive revolution in the field of organization development and change management" (Quinn et al., 2003, qtd. in Cooperrider & Whitney, 2005, p. 1).

AI is defined as a "collaborative and highly participative, system-wide approach to seeking, identifying, and enhancing the 'life-giving forces' that are present when a system is performing optimally in human, economic, and organization terms" (Watkins, Mohr, & Kelly, 2011, p. 22). AI is a relatively new change model that uses positive energy to help people see new possibilities (Bushe, 2009, p. 1) and assists in OD.

Brainstorming

OD is not a quick-fix strategy, but a long-term change effort fully supported by leadership, communicated throughout the organization, includes input from all levels, and is seen as a journey rather than a finite event. It provides long-term impact that should lead to deep and significant change at the heart of the organization (people)—employees participate in identifying the problem and develop possible solutions. Engaging the employees creates an investment in the change process and provides a structure for leading for long-lasting change that meets organizational goals. Thus, OD creates a learning environment in which employees feel valued and are not forced to change but become the change agents (Cady et al., 2010; Rothwell et al., 2010).

Training has a role in every organization. It serves to target a specific need and improve skills or knowledge in a particular area. It should be used as an adjunct to organizational change but does not have the capacity to be the catalyst for organizational change. OD sets forth a process to help an organization determine the change needed/wanted, complete needs assessment(s), determine the data needed to evaluate change, communicate throughout the process, and engage all members at the appropriate levels along the way. It is more holistic in its approach and reach—allowing the entire organization to take stock of its goals and the interventions necessary to meet those goals. It is the 30,000-foot perspective that allows the leaders

to reach all the way down to the ground and create change through deliberate steps with defined metrics along the way.

2.7 Training Evaluation

Evaluation of the intervention is essential to verify the results and show
improvement postintervention. Training is a quick fix or one-time change
that takes only a few hours to a few days. Evaluation of a training event
should be carefully planned and include conversations that establish the
time frames for evaluation, type of data needed to complete the evaluation,
and what participants will be included in the sample. Another critical consideration would be to define the training outcomes and then consider what
evaluation metrics will ascertain if those objectives have been met.

Time frames can vary and should be connected to the outcome that is
being sought. The evaluation can be a point in time or over a few time
frames during the training event. For instance, if the education will train
employees on the use of a new piece of equipment, the evaluation could
include informal assessments during the training, at completion, and then
a few months later to look more closely at skill attainment. A useful framework for developing a training evaluation is to utilize Kirkpatrick's four
levels of evaluation: (a) reaction, (b) learning, (c) behavior, and (d) results
(Kirkpatrick, 1998). Each level considers a specific focus, and the original
model has been updated to include more specifics. "Reaction" evaluation
looks to gain an understanding of how the employees experience the training. The tool could be a quick survey or verbal feedback in the session
conducted by the trainer. The "learning" level evaluates how well the skill or
knowledge was attained. This level would require a skilled observer and the
use of a checklist or competency with specific skill criteria. The "behavior"
evaluation studies the extent to which the employee applied the training
information in their job. Here, the criteria can be evaluated by survey-
ing the supervisor, observing the employee in action, or monitoring data
(identified in advance). The last level, "results," assesses the achievement of
outcomes and support from the organization. The evaluation for this level
should be crafted before the start of training and be connected to the overall outcomes for the new skill, knowledge, or re-education event. It is best
to conduct a summative evaluation at the end of the program to assess the
four levels of evaluation, including Phillips' fifth level, and return on investment (ROI) (Head & Sorensen, 2005; Rothwell et al., 2010). ROI seeks to

connect interventions with outcome metrics that makes improvement clearly definable.

The complexity of the task or skill will also influence the type of evaluation used. In addition, the evaluation of a training event will focus only on the training activities and does not consider wider organizational change efforts or other variables that fall outside the time frame or episode. Usually, a training evaluation falls into the short-term category and is focused on the one intervention/event.

2.8 OD Evaluation

On the other hand, the long-term focus of OD change looks to assess the broader impact of change in a group, department, or organization. This change often focuses on meeting the strategic goals of an organization and re-centering work around the organization's mission. This type of evaluation requires a deliberate planning process and a commitment of time and resources by leadership in order for the change effort to take hold. Resources include those with a financial impact: time, equipment/supplies, and expertise.

Financial considerations need to be discussed early and re-evaluated during the change effort. Gaining input from all parties, from the start, that may need support is crucial to creating an efficient process. Committing to a best practice evaluation will require time from employees as well as leadership. Other needed resources could include the following:

- Identification of evaluation metrics (key performance indicators and balanced scorecard [BSC] development, helping to measure ROI)
- Creation of new digital data gathering avenues
- Creation of new data gathering tools
- New positions or allocation of time within current positions
- Project team creation
- Outreach to stakeholders (inside and outside the organization)
- Space
- Equipment
- Supplies

Considering all the elements that need to be defined, it should be clear that OD evaluation should occur before the start and during each step of the change process as it informs the next phase, improving efficiency. This

ed- definitions of formative & summative

formative (ongoing) process follows each change effort step during the intervention to assure alignment with organizational strategic goals. This is called a "feedback loop" and is a critical element when addressing any change effort. During and after each step, the identified metrics are used to improve the process or communicate progress to goals. For example, in the business case, the team would need to identify a way to collect data on key performance indicators in order to fully assess the employees so they develop a report to pull those data. After the first pull of data, the team gathers to assess what information the report provides. During this meeting, the frontline managers might share that the information does not show efficiency numbers and was not helpful. The team revises the report and decides to meet again after the second data pull to reassess. This feedback loop should occur with any and all parts of the intervention to continually improve efficiency and impact.

real life utility of this ↓ my world- keystoned PSSAs

Finally, it is important to keep evaluating organizational change even after the formal end of the change event. OD consultants will purposefully plan a separation phase to address closing out the formal change effort as well as plan any ongoing evaluation needs. At this point, the internal leaders or consultants should have a clear plan to maintain a streamline feedback loop to continue to the positive results and identify any further needs. OD evaluation does require an outlay of resources as compared to a training event but, if planned correctly, should decrease the need to retool a misdirected change event and focus the team on meeting goals. It requires the involvement of leaders from the start—who are committed to change and willing to see the process through to the end.

how can I teach account- ability in school? real life lessons

Accountability is another consideration often missed in the planning of a change event. Each member of the team is already very busy with many demands on their time. There is a tendency to allow their responsibilities in a project like this slip to the bottom of the task list. In order to keep it a high priority, leadership can assign specific accountability metrics. The participation in and execution of the evaluation assignments should be part of their performance evaluation and be monitored by supervisors in order to assure compliance and the attainment of goals. Leadership can use the accountability metrics as a motivational tool by being transparent with the praise and redirection needed throughout the journey.

Figure 2.1 shows the steps of the Action Research Model created by Kurt Lewin in the 1940s (Warley et al. 2010) and remains the primary model used when developing organizational change. The model addresses worker motivation and performance, conflict in industry, group problem solving, communication, and attitude change (Burnes, 2000).

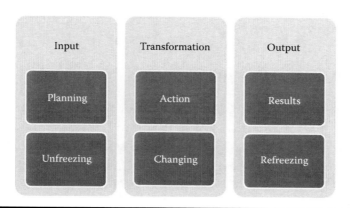

Figure 2.1   Adaptation of the Action Research Model in OD intervention, and the evaluation steps during the intervention. (Adapted from McLean, G. M., Sullivan, R., & Rothwell, W. J. (1995). Evaluation. In W. J. Rothwell & R. Sullivan (Eds.) *Practicing organization development: A guide for consultants*. San Francisco: Jossey-Bass/Pfeffer.)

The Action Research Model is "a framework for diagnosing, implementing, and evaluating a change process" (Egan & Lancaster, 2005, p. 35). This Action Research Model involves a cyclical process of change. The cycle process is illustrated in Figure 2.2. The cycle has several steps, sometimes repeated in a cyclical mode (Rothwell & Sullivan, 2010). These steps are Entry, Start-up, Assessment and Feedback, Action Planning, Intervention, Evaluation, Adoption, and Separation (Rothwell & Sullivan, 2010). The evaluation starts early in the OD intervention and continues throughout as well as after the formal OD change. Since that OD intervention might be subdivided into milestones and might take more time, the evaluation of the OD intervention can be conducted several times. The Action Research Model is very

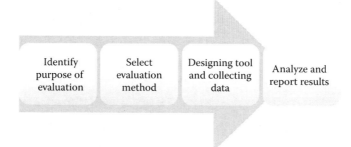

Figure 2.2   Organizational change processes. (Adapted from Manual on training evaluation: Project on improvement of local administration in Cambodia. Retrieved from http://www.jica.go.jp/project/cambodia/0601331/pdf/english/5_TrainingEvaluation.pdf.)

flexible and affords the entire team with opportunities to give feedback and assess the current process.

2.9 Objectives of Training

The aim of both training and OD evaluation is to ensure that the intervention effort meets the planned outcome that had been specified by the consultants and the stockholders ahead of intervention implementation.

Training is an effort that targets a group of people in an industry who need skills or need to be taught new skills that are going to enhance their work experience, develop their personal knowledge and awareness, change attitudes, and increase work productivity. Before evaluating a training program, the consultant needs to be clear about the objectives of conducting the evaluation. Kirkpatrick and Kirkpatrick (2006) specified three reasons for evaluating a training program: (1) to justify the existence and budget of the training department by showing how it contributes to the organization's objectives and goals, (2) to decide whether to continue or discontinue training programs, and (3) to gain information on how to improve future training programs.

2.10 Objectives of OD Evaluation Approach

OD is an intentional action taken to create change in a system and targets a large group of an organization or all employees in the organization. Thus, evaluation in the OD case is to examine the impact of an intervention that aligns with the organization's goal (Cady et al., 2010).

The evaluation of OD intervention as well as the evaluation of the training interventions follows the same evaluation steps as seen in Tool 2.1: identifying the purpose of the evaluation, selecting and evaluating the method, designing an evaluation tool and collecting data, and analyzing and reporting results. They diverge at the start as seen in the overall objective difference between the two approaches. The OD change approach is broader, is deeper, and looks to make systems alternations.

2.11 Business Case: Why Invest and How Will It Be Value Added?

Money will be spent during any solid organizational change effort. The ultimate question will be "Was it worth it?" This may be the most asked question about any event—training or systems change—but only because the data to support answers are missing. If a conscious effort is put into thinking about how the leadership can evidence success, the question becomes easy and a source of pride. The ability to show that the intended result of the intervention has been achieved is likely unachievable without an evaluation throughout, including after the change effort.

The benefits of allotting time for evaluation show up in a variety of places including decreasing mistakes that require additional costs to fix. It may lead to early discovery of any weak areas in the intervention and allow modification of the plan so that it better aligns with business strategy objectives. Also, gathering data from participants helps in identifying their thoughts about the change effort and may bring issues of commitment, morale, and systems dysfunction to light. Furthermore, it assures stockholders and managers that the change has value and has been worth the financial investment (Alzahmi et al., 2013; Head & Sorensen, 2005). It has other long-term benefits for the board and stakeholders in that they are more likely to support this method of change if they can see financial bottom-line impact from the start.

The financial benefits of the OD evaluation can be estimated by doing a cost–benefit analysis by calculating the cost of the change (or training) effort in comparison to the improvements seen in identified metrics: increased customer satisfaction or sales numbers. Financial considerations were discussed earlier in the chapter but bear repeating here as a good project management plan avoids many surprise costs and keeps a change effort in time and on target. Some of the variables to keep in mind are the costs of employee time, materials, consultants (travel and materials), participants' time, and any other anticipated cost. Once the costs are defined, the comparison to potential benefits should begin.

One way to measure success is through the use of a BSC. This may already be in place to measure big-picture metrics but can be adapted for the specific change effort. The BSC was developed by Robert Kaplan and David Norton in 1992 and consists of four areas: (1) financial goals, (2) customer perspective, (3) internal processes, and (4) learning and growth or innovation. Developing a BSC should help any organization to achieve the following:

■ A management tool for organizational development and incentive programs.
■ Give managers a fast, concise, and comprehensive picture of both financial and operational measures.

- Emphasis on organizational vision and long-term success.
- Significant operational areas can be examined to see whether one result may have been achieved at the expense of another, so managers can see the critical operational factors and their interrelationships with current and future performance in mind (Kaplan & Norton, 1992).

The benefits of evaluation efforts can go beyond the financial spreadsheet, and the leadership team should make time to brainstorm how the change will benefit the business (strategic goals) and in turn the ROI. For example, the BSC can provide data on customer service, employee production numbers, or employee morale. Leaders can tie evaluation of the learning experience and the resulting growth from the intervention or the client and participants' perspectives of the intervention. Newby (1992) suggested that by calculating the OD ROI of the intervention, the organization gets a clear insight of the financial benefits of the evaluation portion.

Phillips (1997), in the *Handbook of Training Evaluation and Measurement Methods*, describes one way to calculate the financial benefits from evaluation. Start getting ready by allocating the time and organizational level to do the evaluation and preparing the evaluation instruments. The next step is collecting the data from participants, cleaning the data, and then converting it to a monetary value. The collected data are divided into two main types: first, the tangible data, which can be calculated to find out the ROI of the evaluation, and second, the intangible benefits from the evaluation. In Figure 2.3, Phillips (1997) presents an option for calculating the ROI. Any business case presented

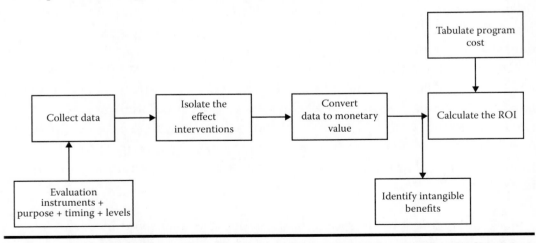

Figure 2.3   ROI calculation. (Adapted from Phillips, J. J. (1997). *Handbook of Training Evaluation and Measurement Methods*, 3rd ed. Houston, TX: Gulf Publishing Company.)

to the executive team should include a detailed calculation of ROI for the change event. Evaluation is often not considered a valuable task because an ROI calculation is missing, which leads to lack of outcome assessment. It is important to remember that intangible benefits are often hard to measure but a critical aspect of any ROI evaluation. Specific effort should occur to identify these intangibles and a metric that in some way creates quantifiable data point(s).

This section provides a cursory review of the possibilities when tying outcomes to change efforts. Regardless of the method used to show value, the edict is clear: evaluation metrics must be identified and then tracked in order to provide leaders with the data needed to evidence success.

2.12 Chapter Summary

This chapter provides an overview of the differences between training objectives and evaluation as compared to the broader scope organizational change evaluation. OD change and the requisite evaluation metrics support long-term benefits to the entire organization. The strategic perspective of change requires that the time spent be worth the expense and each type of intervention provides different benefits. Some takeaways from the chapter include the following:

- OD is a long-term change effort that requires resource investment as compared to short-term training, which has a very different focus but also requires an evaluation component.
- Organizations that commit to determining how evaluation will be used to measure success are more likely to realize their intended results.
- The training evaluation can be conducted fewer times than the OD evaluation.
- Training and change will require a variety of resources, and incorporating evaluation throughout both processes will help avoid misuse of resources and help avoid lack of change adoption.
- Metrics that support evaluation efforts should be identified early and revised as needed.
- The feedback loop is critical in the revision of the plan, allowing participants to be heard as well as improving the long-term efficiency and effectiveness of the project.

2.13 Key Definitions

Evaluation: The evaluation of OD in this chapter is a systematic assessment that is conducted for an ongoing or completed project, program, or policy—its design, implementation and results. The goal is to determine the relevance and fulfillment of objectives, development, efficiency, effectiveness, impact, and sustainability (OECD, 2002).

Formative evaluation: An evaluation is conducted during the intervention to assess whether the intervention is producing the intended results and to modify and align the intervention if there is any mistake or failure (Rothwell, 2014).

Longitudinal: Evaluation occurs after implementation to ensure that the change is ongoing at the organization (Rothwell, 2014).

Organization development: OD is a process of planned change in an organization's culture (Burke, 1994). It is a planned, long-term change effort that uses behavioral science and is managed from the top to increase organizational effectiveness and health processes using behavioral-science knowledge (Beckhard, 1969). It is "a response to change, a complex educational strategy intended to change the beliefs, attitudes, values, and structure of organizations so that they can better adapt to new technologies, markets, and challenges, and the dizzying rate of change itself" (Bennis, 1969, p. 2).

Organization Development Evaluation: "*OD Evaluation* is a set of planned, information-gathering, and analytical activities undertaken to provide those responsible for the management of change with a satisfactory assessment of the effects and/or progress of the change effort" (Beckhard & Harris, 1977, p. 86). It is an ongoing process of data gathering during the intervention effort to assess the alignment of the planned change to the organization's need. In addition, it assures that the intervention producing and sustaining the intended results through three main stages of evaluation during the intervention, at the end of the intervention, and after the intervention (Rothwell, 2014).

Summative evaluation: An evaluation is conducted after the implementation of the change effort to prove that the intervention had produced the planned results (Rothwell, 2014).

Training: Training is defined as the "learning, provided by employers to employees, that is related to their present jobs" (Nadler & Nadler, 1989; Rothwell & Sredl, 2000, p. 9). It is a short-term change effort, or learning intervention that builds on employees' knowledge or skills to meet current or future job requirements (Rothwell & Graber, 2010; Rothwell & Sredl, 2000).

2.14 Tool

Tool 2.1

Answer the questions to help you determine what type of intervention suits the identified problem best.

The assessment column: There may need to be an assessment before determining which option is best. Even if the choice seems clear, an assessment is always a good opportunity to assure all the issues are understood before beginning any intervention.

Problem/Question	Training: Short Term, Skill Oriented, Point in Time (Often)	Assessment: Needs Assessment, Gap Analysis, Growth Gap, SWOT Analysis	Change Effort: Systemic Change at Any Level, New Opportunity for Org Growth
Teaching a new skill, skill-based outcome	XX		
Learning a new piece of equipment functionality	XX		
Competency based	XX		
Poor job performance			
Are you looking for impacts systems with new solutions		XX	XX
Determine why organization is not meeting strategic goals or outcomes		XX	
Investigate causes of low employee morale		XX	XX
Instruction on a new customer service method	XX		

References

Alzahmi, R. A., Rothwell, W. J., Kim, W., & Park, C. H. (2013). A practical evaluation approach for OD intervention. *IJRMEC, 3*(3), 43–65.

Beckhard, R. (1969). *Organizational Development: Strategies and Models*. Reading, MA: Addison-Wesley Pub. Co.

Beckhard, R., & Harris, R. T. (1977). *Organizational Transitions: Managing Complex Change*. Boston: Addison-Wesley Pub. Co.

Bennis, W. (1969). *Organization Development: Its Nature and Prospect*. Boston: Addison-Wesley Pub. Co.

Buckingham, M., & Clifton, D. O. (2001). *Now, Discover Your Strengths*. New York: Free Press.

Burnes, B. (2000). *Managing Change*, 3rd ed. Harlow, England: Financial Times Pearson Educational.

Burke, W. (1994). *Organization Development Process of Learning and Changing*. Reading, MA: Addison-Wesley Publication.

Bushe, G. R. (2000). Advances in appreciative inquiry as an organization development intervention. In Cooperrider, D. L., Sorenson, P. F, Jr., Whitney, D., & Yaeger, T. (Eds.), *Appreciative Inquiry: Rethinking Human Organization toward a Positive Theory of Change* (pp. 113–121). San Francisco: Wiley/Pfeiffer.

Bushe, G. R. (2009). Generativity and the transformational potential of appreciative inquiry. In Zandee, D., Cooperrider, D. L., & Avital, M. (Eds.), *Organizational Generativity: Advances in Appreciative Inquiry* (Volume 3). Amsterdam: Elsevier.

Cady, S. H., Auger, J., Foxon, M. (2010). Situational evaluation. In Rothwell, W. J., Stavros, J. M., & Sullivan, R. L. (Eds.), *Practicing Organization Development: A Guide for Leading Change*, 3rd ed. San Francisco: Pfeiffer.

Cambridge University Press. (2016). Cambridge Online Dictionary Ohio, Retrieved from: dictionary.cambridge.org/us.

Clifton, D., & Harter, J. (2003). Investing in your strengths. In Cameron, K. S., Dutton, J.E., & Quinn, R.E. (Eds.), *Positive Organizational Scholarship: Foundations of a New Discipline* (pp. 111–121). San Francisco: Berrett-Koehler Publishers, Inc.

Coghlan, D., & Claus, J. (2005). Kurt Lewin on reeducation: Foundations for Action Research. *The Journal of Applied Behavioral Science, 41*(4), 444–457. Retrieved November 4, 2010, from ABI/INFORM Global. (Document ID: 930782491).

Cooperrider, D. L., & Srivastva, S. (1987). Appreciative inquiry in organizational life. In Pasmore, W., & Woodman, R. (Eds.), *Research in Organizational Change and Development* (Vol. 1, pp. 129–169). Greenwich, CT: JAI Press.

Cooperrider, D. L., & Whitney, D. (2005). *Appreciative Inquiry: A Positive Revolution in Change*. San Francisco: Berrett-Koehler Publishers, Inc.

Egan, T. M., & Lancaster, C. M. (2005). Comparing appreciative inquiry to action research: OD practitioner perspectives. *Organization Development Journal, 23*(2), 29–49.

French, W. L., & Bell, C. H. (1995). *Organization Development: Behavioral Science Interventions for Organization Improvement*, 5th ed. Englewood Cliffs, NJ: Prentice-Hall.

Head, T. C., & Sorensen, P. F., Jr. (2005). The evaluation of organization development interventions: An empirical study. *Organization Development Journal*, *23*(1), 40–55.

JICA. (n.d.). *Manual of Training Evaluation: Project in Improvement of Administration in Cambodia*. Retrieved from http://www.jica.go.jp/project /cambodia/0601331/pdf/english/5_TrainingEvaluation.pdf

Kaplan, R. S., & Norton, D. P. (1992). The balanced scorecard: Measures that drive performance. *Harvard Business Review*, January–February, 71–79.

Kirkpatrick, D. L. (1998). *Evaluating Training Programs: The Four Levels*. San Francisco: Berrett-Koehler.

Kirkpatrick, D. L., & Kirkpatrick, J. D. (2006). *Evaluating Training Programs: The Four Levels*, 3rd ed. San Francisco: Berrett-Koehler.

McLean, G. M., Sullivan, R., & Rothwell, W. J. (1995). Evaluation. In Rothwell, W. J., & Sullivan, R. (Eds.). *Practicing Organization Development: A Guide for Consultants*. San Francisco: Jossey-Bass/Pfeffer.

Nadler, L., & Nadler, Z. (1989). *Developing Human Resources*, 3rd ed. San Francisco: Jossey-Bass.

Newby, T. (1992). *Training Evaluation Handbook*. San Diego, CA: Pfeiffer & Co.

OECD. (2002). *Evaluation and Aid Effectiveness No. 6—Glossary of Key Terms in Evaluation and Results Based Management (in English, French and Spanish)*. OECD Publishing. doi:10.1787/9789264034921-en-fr

Papanek, M. L. (1973, August). Kurt Lewin and his contributions to modern management theory. *Academy of Management Proceedings*, *1*, 317–322.

Phillips, J. J. (1997). *Handbook of Training Evaluation and Measurement Methods*, 3rd ed. Houston, TX: Gulf Publishing Company.

Quinn, R. E., Camerson, K. S., & Dutton, J. E. (2003). *Positive Organizational Scholarship*. San Francisco: Berrett-Koehler.

Rath, T., & Conchie, B. (2009). *Strengths-Based Leadership*. New York: Gallup.

Rothwell, W. J. (2014). *Appraising organization development and consulting for trainers* [PowerPoint slides].

Rothwell, W. J., & Graber, J. M. (2010). *Competency-Based Training Basics*. East Peoria, IL: Versa Press.

Rothwell, W. J., & Sredl, H. J. (2000). *Workplace Learning and Performance: Present and Future Roles and Competencies*, 3rd ed. Amherst, MA: HRD Press, Inc.

Rothwell, W. J., Stavros, J. M., & Sullivan, R. L. (2010). Organization development and change. In Rothwell, W. J., Stavros, J. M., & Sullivan, R. L. (Eds.), *Practicing Organization Development: A Guide for Leading Change*, 3rd ed. San Francisco: Pfeiffer.

Rothwell, W. J., & Sullivan, R. L. (2010). Change process models. In Rothwell, W. J., Stavros, J. M., Sullivan, R. L., & Sullivan, A. (Eds.), *Practicing Organization Development: A Guide for Leading Change*, 3rd ed., pp. 43–70. San Francisco: Pfeiffer.

Sekerka, L. E., Brumbaugh, A. M., José Antonio, R., & Cooperrider, D. (2006). Comparing appreciative inquiry to a diagnostic technique in organizational change: The moderate effect of gender. *International Journal of Organization Theory and Behavior, 9*(4), 449–489.

Warley, C., Rothwell, W. J., & Sullivan, R. L. (2010). Competencies of OD practitioners. In Rothwell, W. J., & Sullivan, R. L. (Eds.), *Practicing Organization Development*, 3rd ed. San Diego, CA: Pfeiffer.

Watkins, J. M., & Mohr, B. J. (2001). *Appreciative Inquiry: Change at the Speed of Imagination*. San Diego, CA: Jossey-Bass.

Watkins, J. M., Mohr, B. J., & Kelly, R. (2011). *Appreciative Inquiry: Change at the Speed of Imagination*, 2nd ed. Hoboken, New Jersey: John Wiley & Sons.

White, S. R. (2004). *A critical action research approach to curriculum development in a laboratory-based chemical engineering course* (Doctoral dissertation).

Chapter 3

Aligning Evaluation to Organizational Strategy

Maria T. Spencer and Marie Carasco-Saul

Contents

3.1 Introduction

An organization's strategy operationalizes multiple interrelated factors to drive its organization, processes, and people in order to seek and maintain a competitive position in the market. These factors may include the organization's value proposition to customers, its position within the market, components of its business model, and so on. The outcomes can be measured in the form of "strategic" or "key performance indicators" (KPIs), which generally include a combination of financial and nonfinancial measures related to the organization's relative success in the market. An organization development (OD) intervention can be a powerful tool in the effort to produce and maintain the alignment of the organization's human capital with the organization's strategy, because, among other benefits, OD interventions can help organizations facilitate the development of a shared vision and collective buy-in to the organization's goals and strategic imperatives. When an OD intervention is designed to aid in the implementation of organizational strategy, the strategic indicators become important measures of the intervention itself.

Strategic indicators can span the spectrum from simple financial indicators like revenue and expenses through more complex qualitative measures of the organization's capacity to learn and innovate. Meaningful measures should be developed at the start of the intervention and revisited periodically throughout the effort to maintain participants' focus and measure success around key deliverables. This range and the individualized nature of an organization's strategy mean that both the OD intervention and the evaluation efforts must be thoughtfully customized and made meaningful to the sponsor of the OD intervention.

When strategic alignment drives the intervention, the focus will inherently be comprehensive and multifaceted, and the evaluation correspondingly so. With these multiple facets come multiple stakeholders from both inside and outside of the organization, and the measures relevant to each stakeholder group are likely to vary. Stakeholder identification and communication is important with respect to not only continued buy-in to the OD intervention but also the flow of resources and the management of barriers to the desired intervention outcomes. As such, this chapter will outline some key considerations with respect to identifying and communicating with stakeholders, developing accurate, meaningful and actionable measures, identifying resources, overcoming barriers, evaluating the evaluation process, and finally feeding back the results of evaluation.

Tools and activities have been provided at the end of the chapter, and the following case and case discussion are offered to illustrate some of the key considerations in this chapter.

3.2 Chapter Overview

This chapter will provide guidance, information, and resources that the practitioner can use to help align the evaluation of OD interventions with the broader organizational strategy. The chapter will cover the following areas:

- Stakeholder identification and communication
- Strategy alignment
- What to measure and how
- Resource identification
- Process evaluation and management of feedback
- How appraising an OD effort can benefit the organization

3.3 Business Case

Mike Jones, the CEO of Options Media, Inc., noted with great concern that the trend in consumer media was shifting away from physical media like DVDs toward streaming online media from devices like smartphones and tablets. Options Media had an engineering services business model through which they contracted with larger companies to develop the technology that enabled physical media playback devices, like DVD players. Jones recognized the importance of adapting the company's strategy in order to keep the company relevant to the changing market so, he called his leadership team together to work through the plan for change.

The change effort did not start off with much consensus. Jones was the team's visionary; he saw the big picture and challenged his team to do the same. But although the team recognized the warning signs in the market and verbally expressed a willingness to change. It was difficult to let go of roles and processes that had worked well for so long. The change required entirely new ways of working, a new position in the value chain, new products, revenue models, customer relationships—the list went on. The company's whole business model would need to change in response to the new strategy.

3.3.1 Varying Response to the Change

Each of the senior leaders had their own questions and reactions regarding the change. There were questions about resources, about what the shift toward streaming media would mean to the company's customers and revenues, and about how the change in strategy would alter the authority and accountability structure of the leadership team. The director of human resources adopted a tactical focus on what the change would mean to his current staffing, training, and personnel management systems. The chief information officer took a wait-and-see approach, making it known that, while she understood the need for change, she did not believe the company was well positioned for it and presumed this change effort would fail. The chief financial officer asked many questions, grilling the CEO for specifics regarding the cost and eventual payoff of the change initiative before he would buy-in. The vice president of sales was most conflicted of all, having noted the changes in the market for some time, but with a keen awareness of the risk the company was undertaking by changing their competitive strategy—especially considering the rapid rate of technological change in their industry.

3.3.2 OD Intervention as a Path toward Consensus

The leadership team elected to engage an OD consultant to help the organization work through the change. Specifically, the OD consultant was asked to help the company build consensus for the new direction at all levels of the organization and to help the team develop shared goals and agreed-upon metrics of success. The OD consultant met with the senior leadership team and then other members of the organization individually and asked open-ended questions about the organization, the proposed change initiative, and the future of the organization. When finished with the interviews, she fed the information back, highlighting the major themes and emphasizing the areas where the organization had a shared vision, and where it did not. As the team processed the information, the OD consultant asked them to relate each of the themes to the organization's various stakeholders, both internal and external. Individuals from across the organization contributed to a list of stakeholders that included customers, other units within the company, suppliers, the workforce, and their families. When asked how they would know when they were successful in their new direction, responses were mixed; some suggested net revenue, others suggested when the first new streaming media product went to market, and still others had no response at all, looking directly to Johnson for indications of success.

3.3.3 Facilitating the Development of Metrics

The OD consultant took the feedback from stakeholders and the partial list of metrics and facilitated a session with members from each of the units. A representative from a key customer was also invited to participate. Over the course of two hours, the OD consultant facilitated a brainstorming session where the members of the organization developed performance objectives for each imperative of the new strategy. Strategic imperatives were then matched to stakeholder groups, and the stakeholders' primary value (both tangible and intangible) out of each imperative were quantified. Once the team had agreed on what success looked like, they were able to work backward and identify the contributions each unit and team needed to make in support of the desired outcomes. The results of the facilitated session were communicated throughout the rest of the organization and comments and feedback was encouraged. A final list of "desired results" was compiled and would be used at completion of the intervention to measure the success of the initiative. The senior leadership team agreed that this process helped them to develop a shared vision and to obtain the buy-in of their team for the new ways of working.

3.3.4 Facilitating Evaluation

The OD consultant cautioned the team that this set of metrics, which focused on the end goal of the intervention, was only part of the information the team could measure as part of the evaluation. She emphasized the importance of *formative* evaluation, which would occur at various points throughout their efforts to measure progress, check for strategic alignment, and determine what efforts are yielding desired results. She also recommended a *summative* evaluation immediately following what the organization deemed to be the "end" of the intervention. This summative evaluation

would involve the collection of information—especially new knowledge—
that had been developed throughout the course of the intervention. This
new knowledge would be particularly important to the organization's efforts
to keep their strategy in tune with market demands.

3.3.5 *Appraisal and Strategic Alignment*

With all of this in mind, the team decided to take a baseline of where they
were with some of the metrics developed during the facilitated session so that
they could appraise their progress throughout the initiative based on where
they were starting from. They elected to use a "Balanced Scorecard" approach
and monitor four primary focus areas: financial performance, customer
satisfaction, operational effectiveness, and organizational learning and growth
(Kaplan & Norton, 1996). The OD consultant played the role of facilitator as
the company determined which strategic objectives to keep the closest tabs
on, and she encouraged them to keep the list manageable so that they did not
dilute their focus by trying to pay attention to too many things at once. The
team appointed a small multiunit team to monitor the results and communicate brief status updates to the rest of the organization on a biweekly basis.

In negotiating their next steps with the OD consultant, the organization
decided that it would handle the formative evaluation but asked for another
facilitated session for the summative evaluation. The consultant agreed and,
at the same time, negotiated limited rights to use the results of the intervention and evaluation in her marketing.

Case Discussion:

- Identify the primary steps that the OD consultant helped the company
  walk through relative to the intervention and evaluation, beginning with
  the development of a shared vision among the leadership team.
- Review the strategic importance of both formative and summative
  evaluation.
- What barriers might the organization encounter in trying to execute on
  this multifaceted appraisal? What things can they do to guard against
  implementation barriers?
- How might the evaluation process differ when the intervention is based
  on a proactive, rather than a reactive change?
- How will the organization know if the OD intervention has been a success, both in the short and the long term?

3.4 Stakeholder Identification and Communication

Foundational to the success of any OD intervention—and subsequent evaluation—is the accuracy of the organization diagnosis. This process requires collecting the right information about an organization system and the people within it (Alderfer, 1980). It is a recursive process that goes from entry, data collection, and feedback during an intervention as new information, data, and resources present themselves. For this reason, the process of diagnosis is continual, and should not be considered finalized when moving into the other phases of an OD intervention. This is not to say that the formal diagnosis phase should not be curtailed; otherwise, the practitioner would not progress with their client work. Consultants manage the relationship between the system and the data collection. In fact, this system "can be a source of advice about the content and design of feedback" (Alderfer, 1980). Therefore, it is imperative that the practitioner identify key stakeholders, decision makers, loci of power, and how best to communicate within the organization system. At the end of this chapter, we provide a checklist to help identify key stakeholders in any organization system.

Stakeholders can include any individuals or groups that affect the achievement of goals in an organization (Freeman, 1984). This definition is only the beginning, since a stakeholder can essentially be anyone except those who cannot affect the firm or are not affected by it. However, "[n]arrow views of stakeholders are based on the practical reality of limited resources, limited time and attention, and limited patience of managers for dealing with external constraints. In general, narrow views of stakeholders attempt to define relevant groups in terms of their direct relevance to the firm's core economic interests" (Mitchell et al., 1997, p. 857).

The challenge for OD professionals is to find the middle ground, which can be aided by your points of contact in the liaison system. "Depending on the nature of the system, the liaison system may be an individual, a series of individuals, or a group" (p. 461). This liaison system is a stakeholder of itself and simultaneously your first source of information regarding other stakeholders within and external to the client system. However, they should not be the only source. Stakeholder identification requires taking a broad brush approach with data collection, including but not limited to the following:

- Formal and informal conversations
- Interviews
- Observations

■ Archival data
■ Surveys

The practitioner would do well to uncover how decisions are made, procedures are approved, and the relationship between those making those decisions are those charged with implementing them. Stakeholders will be key to help determine the metrics as they relate to the specific data or measures used to assess the outcome of an intervention (Cheung-Judge & Holbeche, 2011).

Communication of findings can be problematic if not defined and agreed to early in contracting. Given the myriad of stakeholders in the client system, it is important to clarify who should be informed, what they need to know, how they'd like the information presented, and how often. Forms of communication include scheduling of meetings (virtual and face to face), e-mails, or phone calls and alike. The content of that communication includes providing feedback, gaining clarification on a matter, alerting the client to an issue, and so on. It should be noted that there are indirect forms of communication from both the client and the practitioner that have an impact on the intervention. Examples include timeliness of responses, the use of silence, avoidance, delegation, types of emotional responses, ambiguity, and other ways in which the communication is conveyed. A checklist is included on stakeholder identification and suggestions on communication in Section 3.12.

3.5 Strategy Alignment

Much like the evaluation, the OD intervention should be reflective of the organization's overall strategy, either on the whole, or specific to one of its parts (e.g., reducing turnover in the Customer Service department to support the organization's strategy of leading its industry in customer service). The alignment of the evaluation with the organization's strategy will depend on the alignment of the OD intervention with the organization's strategy, but with proper attention to this critical detail, the evaluation process can help the OD facilitator and the organization connect the outcomes of the OD intervention to the execution of their competitive strategy.

It is worth noting that the term *strategy* often engenders visions of the executive leadership team, or maybe even the company's "secret sauce," but in reality, the entire organization's workforce is critical to the deployment of strategy. Successful execution of the competitive strategy requires effective function within and across the organization's departments, and it is these functional and cross-functional areas that enable the organization's performance. As such, the OD intervention and the evaluation needs should maintain a holistic view of strategy and consider measures that reach deep into the organization's layers to account for these important functions and cross-functions.

3.5.1 Strategy Execution and the Workforce

Individuals throughout the organization—and not just within the C-suite—should be aware of the overall strategy, as well as how their unit and department fits in and contributes to the success of the organization. The desired strategic outcomes should be the foundation of the OD intervention and provide the framework for the development of process and performance goals relative to both internal and external stakeholders. It is particularly important to align the goals of individuals with the goals of the organization, as job requirements, resources, metrics, training, and so on, will have an effect on behavior and ultimately on performance. Especially when the OD intervention is related to a change in organization strategy, it is important to realign existing goals, metrics, and other performance drivers with the new direction.

3.5.2 Purposeful Units and Unit Goals

Kaplan and Norton (1996) noted the importance of ensuring that the goals and workings of the firm's business units be aligned with the overarching organizational strategy. Strategic alignment initiatives present the opportunity for organizations to examine any unit separations to see if they are justified by any operational or business rationale. Unit designations should ultimately map to the organization's goals, such that any business unit separations are made with the organization's overall goals (and not any individual unit's interests) in mind. If unit designations and separations are part of the OD intervention and evaluation effort, take care to define the business unit's role in furthering the overall organization's strategic goals, enumerating any unit-level goals based on overall organizational objectives.

3.5.3 Strategy and Goal Alignment

Inherent to the alignment of strategy and goals at all levels of the organization is the subsequent alignment of performance metrics. Although an organization should be careful not to create a "moving target" when it comes to employee performance, shifts in goals and competitive strategy should be reflected in how the workforce is evaluated and rewarded. There are many ways to view metrics, though most approaches roughly break measures down between *primary*, indicating the ultimate goal or result desired, and *advanced*, indicating the things that need to happen in order for the ultimate goal or result to be realized (Frost, 2000). The advanced metrics are derived from these ultimate goals, based on the behavior and performance factors which are critical to their successful realization (Frost, 2000). Organizations may look at a number of primary and advanced performance indicators—both internal and external—to track indications of success in strategic priority areas. *Internal metrics*, which are likely to be advanced measures, may include operational measures, such as:

- Quality control outcomes
- Production efficiency
- Turnover in the workforce (and so on)

External metrics, which are typically primary measures, often align with strategic goals such as:

- Market share
- Competitive position
- Customer satisfaction

These strategic measures—both internal and external—may also be broken down into KPIs, or measurable outcomes that are indicative of strategic performance as defined by the organization.

3.6 Developing KPIs: What to Measure and How

KPIs are metrics designed to provide snapshots of critical information for the organization. They can reveal information about the organization's market position and financial performance as well as about various workforce factors, like skill levels, turnover, and productivity (Winkler, 2005). Most organizations will use a variety of KPIs to develop a comprehensive view of multiple factors critical to the organization's success. KPIs may be balanced between internal workforce and profitability factors and external market share and product performance measures.

The value of KPIs lies in their ability to connect strategy to performance in finite, measurable ways that can be closely tracked by the organization. Ideally, KPIs offer information on a few actionable measures so as to guide an organization's leadership in the pursuit of strategic objectives. This means that KPIs need to be accurately selected and deliberately tracked so that the information can serve as a credible management tool. Additionally, for KPIs to be valuable, they must be accurately matched to performance variables within the organization's control. For example, an organization should be careful to differentiate between performance outcomes that are related to operational variables and not environmental variables like economic ups or downs, seasonality, weather, and so on.

When determining KPIs, an organization may want to strike a balance between leading and lagging indicators (Winkler, 2005). Leading indicators have predictive value, and lagging indicators provide definitive information about results and outcomes (financial performance, market share, cost control, etc.). Likewise, KPIs that track information from a variety of internal and external sources (e.g., workforce, market, supply chain, and financial indicators) are likely to have a more complete picture of what is happening inside and outside the organization and may be able to draw important correlations between the data. There is likely to be some trial and error involved in developing a final list of KPIs and the list is worthy of ongoing evaluation to ensure both fit with strategic priorities and accurate measure of desired information.

To develop KPIs (Rothwell, 2013):

- Identify the organization's internal and external stakeholders and develop goals around relevant stakeholder priorities.
- Determine the primary and advanced measures that align with your organization's strategic goals.
- Identify performance criteria critical to delivering on strategic goals, considering both internal and external measures.
- Determine which individuals and departments can influence desired organizational performance outcomes and establish appropriate goals and rewards.
- Choose a few of the most important performance criteria (internal and external) to track and monitor.
- For staff: relate the KPIs to the organization's strategy and offer training on the use of KPIs as a management tool.

The development of KPIs can take place within the context of an OD intervention if the principles of OD underpin the process. This means that the process must include input from all levels of the organization such that staff are "bought in" and the senior leaders are champions for the value of the KPIs. Assuming this foundation is properly laid, the KPIs can inform other human resource development areas, including job descriptions, staff goals, and so on.

3.7 Resource Identification

In an ideal world, projects would have unlimited budgets with unlimited access to stakeholders and all other resources required for a successful intervention. Moreover, "sometimes, unrealistic expectations are implicitly established for planning in terms of both the quality and quantity of [strategic planning systems] outputs" (King, 1983, p. 275). However, organizations are often challenged to work within limited budgets under specific time constraints that lead to limited availability to key stakeholders. Yet, there some resources critical to the practitioner's ability to adequately evaluate the strategic alignment of an OD evaluation that should be part of every intervention. These resources come from four key perspectives—financial, customer, process, and organizational perspectives—as displayed in Tool 3.2, the resource identification checklist. Within these perspectives, Cheung-Judge and Holbeche (2011) suggest that the following kinds of data are needed for evaluation:

- Hard data—statistics, ROI, turnover rates, and so on
- Soft data—survey data, customer feedback
- Energy data—enthusiasm about proposed change
- Readiness and capability data—on those implementing
- Political—understanding how power groups may support or block the intervention and the names of key people to help with the implementation of the intervention
- Competency data—ability to sustain the change
- External data—stakeholders outside the organization
- Competitor—comparison and how change will help or hinder
- Professional—function specific information to change effort

A checklist titled *Determining Resources for Aligning Evaluation to Organizational Strategy* (Tool 3.2) has been included in Section 3.12 to aid in this process.

3.8 Process Evaluation

The chapter thus far has focused on evaluation of the goals of an OD initiative. Evaluation may also be applied to the process, and King (1983) provided 12 elements as part of a direct approach to evaluating a strategic planning system, including the following:

- The effectiveness of planning
- The relative worth of the strategic planning system
- The role and impact of the strategic planning system
- The performance of plans, the relative worth of strategy
- The adaptive value of the strategic planning system
- The relative efficiency
- The adequacy of resources
- The allocation of planning resources
- The appropriateness of planning goals

King (1983) noted that understanding the process and its elements is an important first step in designing a valid evaluation. Notably, though, the evaluation should be driven by the initiative's objectives, and not on analysis of the data alone (Cheung-Judge & Holbeche, 2011). This is important because of the wide variability between organizations, contexts, and change initiatives, and because the evaluation of OD interventions should include a mix of subjective and objective measures that are relevant to the organization and its stakeholders so that they maintain ownership of the process. It is important to understand that Cheung-Judge and Holbeche (2011) highlight that the evaluation phase in an intervention is often influenced by the theoretical framework(s) of the individuals leading the change initiative, and these frameworks—or theories about why problems exist and how to address them—will influence the goals, process, and evaluation of an OD intervention.

3.9 Feedback during Evaluation

Feedback on strategy alignment can take many forms. Common approaches include using a presentation, a formal report, samples of raw data, as well as analysis and synthesis of findings. As it relates to aligning evaluation to organizational strategy, Liedtka and Rosenblum (1996) recommend an Appreciative Inquiry approach that acknowledges and shares the voice of the stakeholders as a means of encouraging widespread ownership and empowerment with respect to the change initiative. The idea is to provide true and appropriate representation of the thoughts, feelings, concerns, and recommendations of those from whom data were collected, both to make their voice heard and to share information about the intervention as freely and widely as possible so as to build engagement and transparency.

Additionally, feedback may contain broad reflections on what Weisbord (1976) suggested from diagnostic questions on two levels:

- How big a gap is there between formal and informal systems (this speaks to the fit between individual and organization)?
- How much discrepancy is there between "what is" and "what ought to be" (this highlights the fit between organization and environment)?

3.10 Chapter Summary

Strategic alignment is important to organizational performance because an organization's strategy is the basis of its value proposition to customers and the foundation of many of its core goals and processes. OD interventions themselves, as well as any related evaluation efforts, should be designed with the organization's overall goals and strategies in mind. Members of the organization at all levels are critical to the successful deployment of strategy and there should be broad awareness of strategic imperatives and alignment between individuals' jobs and performance measures with overall organizational goals and measures.

KPIs can help the organization evaluate its performance in many areas of strategy. Kaplan and Norton (1996) popularized the "balanced scorecard" approach to developing and tracking metrics across functional units and between leading and lagging indicators representing the firm's performance in a number of ways, financial and otherwise. The balanced scorecard approach to strategic evaluation can help organizations view their performance holistically and consider more than short-term financial or economic measures.

It is critical to engage as many stakeholders as possible and appropriate with respect to the OD intervention and its evaluation. Generating the measures themselves is a critical step to the evaluation and should include a number of formative and summative measures that are both subjective and objective, based on the context within the organization and the voices of its stakeholders. The results of the evaluation should be shared with all relevant stakeholders and throughout the organization to promote engagement and buy-in to the intervention. Ultimately, an effective evaluation will include actionable information that aids in the overall facilitation of the OD intervention and provides the various stakeholders with evidence of the intervention's impact.

3.11 Application to the Workforce

- A change in strategy may have many benefits and costs beyond financial performance. Some changes in strategy may cost the organization money in the short term, but yield important consumer intelligence or position the company for future profitability and growth. A well thought-out evaluation will help the organization balance multiple variables over various timelines, according to its strategy.
- The evaluation effort should start before the change effort begins so as to record a baseline of the organization, and to strengthen the change effort with appropriate measures and attention to necessary stakeholders.
- The evaluation may have different levels of focus in the different stages of evolution, based on whether the change is proactive versus reactive (to an organizational deficit). A proactive change may focus more heavily on the results and longitudinal evaluations, whereas an organization correcting a deficit may focus more heavily on the formative and summative evaluations in order to use the new knowledge created to make operational improvements.
- There are barriers and expenses associated with the evaluation process. Specifically, leadership may change, participants may lose interest in the change effort, the evaluation effort may fall behind other priorities, individuals may figure out how to "fudge" evaluation results to maximize financial rewards, the resources supporting the effort (personnel or financial) may dwindle or dry up, and so on.

3.12 Tools

Below are two tools that can be used in the early stages of an OD intervention to ensure alignment to organization strategy. These tools are designed to be used within the context of an OD intervention and may help members of the organization (1) identify key stakeholders who should be actively engaged during the change initiative and (2) collect information that will aid in shaping the evaluation.

Tool 3.1: Aligning Evaluation to Organizational Strategy Stakeholder Identification Checklist

Directions: Use the following questions to identify key stakeholders in the organization. During the early phases of your consultations with the client, particularly the contracting/entry stage, these questions will allow you to clarify the business direction, identify the power structure, and potential roadblocks. These questions are based on Rothwell (2013) and can be strategically asked throughout the intervention process.

Purpose	Questions
Clarify the business direction	• What are the goals of the intervention?
Identify power structure	• Who in the organization would be supportive of this intervention? Why? • Who within the organization determines organizational priorities?
Identify who will be involved	• What are the steps required to obtain approval for a new initiative?
Identify roadblocks	• Who in the organization would be supportive of this intervention? Why? • Who in the organization has the authority to stop any process or change a policy?
Benchmark expectations of previous efforts	• What was the response within the organization (by department, and by Fair Labor Standards Act [FLSA] status) to the last major top-down change? • What would cause an organization-wide initiative to fail?
Understand how things get done	• How are changes communicated in the organization? • Is there a place in the organization that is often used to pilot new initiatives?

Key Activities to Identify Stakeholders:

- Anonymous surveys
- Focus groups
- Observations
- Archival documents and data
- Informal conversations
- Formal and informal meetings
- Stakeholder list provided by the client

Tool 3.2: Determining Resources for Aligning Evaluation to Organizational Strategy Checklist

Directions: Use the following four categories of resources noted in the header of this worksheet as a guide during the entry phase to determine your access to resources. Check the box or fill in the blank for each question in the column category (use a blank sheet for additional workspace).

Financial Perspective— Stakeholder Value on Financial Outcomes	Customer Perspective— Presentation to Customers	Process Perspective— Areas to Excel	Organizational Perspective— Sustaining the Change
What is the budget for the intervention? More specifically, for the evaluation? Budget $_____	What are the customer-specific goals (e.g., reduce dissatisfaction, improve retention, increase referrals)? Goal: Goal: Goal:	What are the units of measurement? How are they operationalized? Measure: Measure: Measure: Measure:	What limits, if any, will you have by way of access to information in this checklist (e.g., time, access to personnel)? Limitations:

(Continued)

Financial Perspective— Stakeholder Value on Financial Outcomes	Customer Perspective— Presentation to Customers	Process Perspective— Areas to Excel	Organizational Perspective— Sustaining the Change
What are the financial goals (e.g., lower cost, increase profitability, increase revenue, etc.)? Goal: Goal:	Is there customer survey-feedback data? ☐ Yes ☐ No	What is the level of evaluation (e.g., Behavior/Attitude changes, Organization Profitability, Learning, Stakeholder Satisfaction)? Evaluation by: a. b. c.	How important is evaluation to the organization? ☐ Important ☐ Somewhat important ☐ Not important
How is risk hedged? By: _____	How will changes in product offering be communicated if new products are added and some products are eliminated (social media strategy, etc.)? By: _____	How will the strategy be operationalized by different functions in the business? By: _____	What is the order of priorities on this checklist? Priority #1: Priority #2: Priority #3: What are the appropriate milestones? Milestone: Milestone: Milestone:

(*Continued*)

Financial Perspective— Stakeholder Value on Financial Outcomes	Customer Perspective— Presentation to Customers	Process Perspective— Areas to Excel	Organizational Perspective— Sustaining the Change
What are the historical performance trends (e.g., statistics, ROI, turnover rates, etc.)? Trend: Trend: Trend:	What information does the organization desire to have about customers that they don't currently have? a. b. c.	What are the short- vs. long-term strategies under evaluation? Short term: Long term:	Who is part of the liaison system? Who within the organization will help with the data analysis and feedback presentation? Contact a: Contact b:
What are the reporting systems in place for planning, budgeting and allocations, etc.? 1. 2. 3.	Are there trends in the industry currently or projected to affect customer patterns? 1. 2. 3.	Are there planned changes in the areas of efficiency (e.g., reduce waste, increase quality), and what is the metric? ☐ Change ☐ No changes Metric(s): _____	In what ways and how frequent will communication take place? ☐ Frequent ☐ Infrequent Timing: _____

3.13 Activity

Feasibility—Determining Readiness for Evaluation

The first step in aligning evaluation with organization strategy is to determine the feasibility and readiness for the process. Since strategy efforts can either occur system-wide, or within specific departments, divisions, or product groups within the organization, the resources required will vary, but can be scaled. The following appraisal activity will assist both internal practitioners and external consultants to determine the current and required bandwidth for strategy evaluation. From an action research perspective, this should be done during a diagnosis phase.

Whenever possible, go to the source. Begin by clarifying with the source of the strategy initiative, or their representatives, the reasons for the initiative, expected outcomes, and the type of resources they are willing to provide to see the process through. This is also the time to identify the team that will be involved in the initiative(s), and their respective responsibilities. Equally important is an understanding of limitations regarding what the organization is unwilling to do (i.e., unwilling to incentivize participation). The practitioner should also take this time to discuss their role in the process, how the initiative fits within the balanced scorecard, and how and when will be collected and shared.

Key Questions

Who is the source of the initiative?
Who are the team members? Responsibilities?
Expected outcome(s) of initiative:
   a.
   b.
   c.
Company committed resources include the following:
   a.
   b.
   c.
Organization's expressed limitations:
   a.
   b.
   c.
   d.

Ways the initiative fit with balanced scorecard:
  a.
  b.
  c.

Operationalize the goals and outcomes

- The expected outcomes need to be operationalized with metrics and key performance indications.
- Once defined, these metrics should be validated by the source of the strategy, or the representative of the initiative and placed within the framework of the balanced scorecard.
- This step should not be skipped as it will be foundational to identifying the resources required to implement and evaluate the strategy.

Key Question

How can the goals and outcomes be operationalized?
Operationalized outcomes:
  a.
  b.
  c.

Use cautious optimism with the availability of resources. More often than not, strategy initiatives are outside the scope of daily operations. From the personnel involvement standpoint, the practitioner should be cautious with expectations of availability of those involved and should obtain insight from the team(s) involved on what is needed to accomplish each of the operationalized goals and KPIs.

Key Question

How involved will representatives from the organization be in this project?
Organization input on how to achieve success:
  a.
  b.
  c.

Data collection, evaluation and feedback. Additional caution should be taken with data collection, evaluation, and communicating feedback. The practitioner should not undertake either step alone. If possible, there should be a team designated for each of these steps, with a timeline.

Key Question

Who in the organization will assist with data collection and evaluation?
Name and Title:
Name and Title:

Take the temperature. The organization may not be prepared to take action on the evaluation results of the strategic initiative. On the one hand, there may be a lot of momentum in getting the process started, but little enthusiasm for follow-through on possible negative results. The practitioner should ask questions around previous initiatives, specifically how data were gathered and how feedback was managed. If there were no such initiatives, questions should focus on power dynamics, decision makers, and location of innovations. If the need for strategic evaluation is not present, the need will have to be generated by the leadership possibly with a gap analysis that emphasizes the desired state. If the leadership is unwilling to do so, it is unlikely that the evaluation efforts will be successful.

Key Questions

How have initiatives such as this been managed in the past?
Who was involved?
Was it successful? Why or why not?

Once all of the aforementioned steps are taken, then the practitioner can then determine the feasibility of evaluation as part of the strategy alignment.

3.14 Key Definitions

Alignment: "Organizational alignment is the practice of aligning a company's strategy, operation, culture, and people behaviors with the central theme of the company" (Ferrara, 2013, p. 132).

Balanced scorecard: mechanism for strategy implementation that aids in measuring business unit strategy and results against the organization's strategy and goals. The scorecard goes beyond financial measures to include customer, operation, and the capacity of the organization to learn (Kaplan & Norton, 1996).

Competitive advantage: the degree to which the resources, capabilities, or positioning in the market are more effective, efficient, or otherwise attractive than the offerings of others in the same marketplace. Competitive advantage suggests that consumers elect the products and services of its possessor over other, less desirable options.

Key performance indicators: a core set of metrics that are indicative of the organization's overall effectiveness.

Organization strategy: the purposeful allocation of resources and effort in pursuit of a competitive advantage in the desired market.

Stakeholder: "Stakeholders are constituencies who are affected, voluntarily or involuntarily, by the actions taken by an organization, such as a corporation" (Darity, 2008, p. 85).

References

Alderfer, C. P. (1980). The methodology of organizational diagnosis. *Professional Psychology, 11*(3), 459.

Cheung-Judge, M., & Holbeche, L. (2011). *Organization Development: A Practitioner's Guide for OD and HR*. London: Kogan Page.

Darity, W. A. (2008). Stakeholders. In Darity, W.A. (Ed.). *International Encyclopedia of the Social Sciences*. (Vol. 8, pp. 85–86). Detroit, MI: MacMillian Reference USA, Retrieved May 10th, 2015, from URL http://go.galegroup.com/ps/i.do?id=G ALE%7CCX3045302584&v=2.1&u=psucic&it=r&p=GVRL&sw=w&asid=68fe1c8b 32944b6df2ef5c2161818f1a

Ferrara, M. H. (2013). Aligning the organization and culture. In Ferrara, M. H. (Ed.). *Gale Business Insights Handbook of Cultural Transformation*. (pp. 131–139). Detroit, MI: Gale Business Insights. Retrieved May 10th, 2015 from URL http://go.galegroup.com/ps/i.do?id=GALE%7CCX2759200020&v=2.1&u=psucic&it =r&p=GVRL&sw=w&asid=8501b2a62c836056138616581033f7ab

Freeman, R. E. (1984) *Strategic Management: A Stakeholder Approach*. Boston: Pitman.

Frost, B. (2000). *Measuring Performance*. Dallas, TX: Measurement International.

Kaplan, R., & Norton, D. (1996). *The Balanced Scorecard: Translating Strategy into Action*. Boston: Harvard Business School Press.

King, W. R. (1983). Evaluating strategic planning systems: Summary. *Strategic Management Journal (Pre-1986), 4*(3), 263.

Liedtka, J., & Rosenblum, J. (1996). Shaping conversations: Making strategy, managing change. *California Management Review, 39*(1), 141–157.

Mitchell, R. K., Agle, B. R., & Wood, D. J. (1997). Toward a theory of stakeholder identification and salience: Defining the principle of who and what really counts. *Academy of Management Review, 22*(4), 853–886.

Rothwell, W. R. (2013). *Appriasing Organization Development.* Personal Collection of William Rothwell, The Pennsylvania State University, State College, PA.

Weisbord, M. R. (1976). Organizational diagnosis: Six places to look for trouble with or without a theory. *Group & Organization Studies, 1*(4), 430–447.

Winkler, H. (2005). Developing KPIs at southern company. *Strategic HR Review,* Z4(4), 28–31. doi:10.1108/14754390580000804

Chapter 4

Planning the Evaluation

Ji Won Park

Contents

4.1 Introduction

The organization development (OD) evaluation process considers two key aspects: (1) demonstrating the success of the OD process and (2) offering valuable feedback to organizational members about the OD process. Such information helps those who are involved in the OD process ensure what changes have been accomplished and determine the readiness to move on to the next step. Thus, OD evaluation should be systematically aligned with each phase of the OD intervention. Planning is the initial action in OD evaluation, and it informs the rest of the steps. Without it, most OD and, in turn, the evaluation processes will fall short of expectations. This chapter focuses on the importance of OD evaluation planning and essential tasks that those who participate in organization change should focus on during the planning stage.

4.2 Overview

This chapter will provide practical and substantive knowledge and tactics for planning effective OD evaluation. The chapter will cover the following areas:

- How is an OD approach distinguishable from change management?
- Why is planning the evaluation critical in OD?
- When is OD evaluation planning conducted?
- What should occur in the OD evaluation planning step?

What has to be examined for the evaluation is a profound issue that should be determined in the planning phase. If there exists ambiguity about what the OD effort evaluates, the evaluation would be like a ship adrift on the vast ocean with no focus and confusion among the organization's members. If the goals and targets for OD evaluation are clear, an OD consultant can assist the organization in producing valuable information that can support further strategic actions.

4.3 Business Case

ABC company, an information technology (IT) engineering company in New York, which is considered the best in its field, started to lose profits after facing a serious economic downturn in the IT engineering industry. To help them identify ways to address the downturn and turn around profits, the company hired consultants for 3 months to carry out an organizational change effort. At the first meeting, the company's CEO emphasized the urgent need to identify ways to meet the changing needs of the industry and recover productivity and profits.

The consultants led a team that worked through the identification of potential root causes, appropriate interventions to address the issues, metrics to assess the outcomes of the intervention (tied to strategic goals), and a communication plan. They launched a comprehensive OD intervention with the employees, managers, and executives after determining that the employees' engagement and overall trust in the organizational decisions were the two most serious issues.

After the 3-month interventions, the consultants assessed the interventions by looking at absenteeism and turnover data. The consultants conducted a survey to determine the extent of the employees' engagement, their attitudes, and openness to the company's goals and mission. The data were gathered and analyzed in hopes it would identify the cause of the issues and show improvement in the aforementioned areas.

The consultants reported the evaluation results to the CEO during the final phase. However, after hearing the results, the CEO mused for a while and said, "It looks like everything has improved, but I'm not sure that the data actually helps us understand the issues or that there is a true enhancement in employee engagement. It seems that the employees are still very negative regarding the company's decisions. Also, I see improvement from the survey data but no significant increase in the company's productivity and profits. Ultimately there is a mismatch and I do not trust the results."

Case Questions

■ Why do you think the company's CEO did not accept the evaluation results?
■ What do you think about the consultant's choices in the evaluation process? Discuss the aspects you think they conducted well and those they conducted poorly.
■ What opportunities may have been missed in the evaluation planning?
■ What could the consultants have done differently to make the CEO believe their evaluation results?

4.4 Why Is an OD Approach Distinguishable from Change Management?

Planning the evaluation is the initial step in OD evaluation, but in reality, it is the first step in the OD process. Many practitioners misunderstand the pivotal role evaluation planning should take in the change process. It does not solely follow the intervention. It must be defined in advance of the intervention and be aligned with the objectives and goals so that the team can make an accurate judgment about whether the intervention has been successfully implemented as intended. In an OD approach, each member of the team has input, when an appropriate intentional procedure should be in place to solidify ideas and feedback results. The planning activities must consider how each group is engaged and then how each goal can be measured. The unique nature of OD intervention differs from the change management approach in that evaluation is completed and fed back after each step.

In contrast, in change management, managers and executives identify, decide, and steer change in a top-down approach. One of the best-known change management approaches is Kotter's (1996) eight-step process:

a. Establishing a sense of urgency
b. Forming a powerful guiding coalition
c. Creating a vision
d. Communicating the vision
e. Empowering others to act on the vision
f. Planning for and creating short-term wins
g. Consolidating improvements and producing still more change
h. Institutionalizing new approaches

This approach makes suggestions for change without significant input from the average employee base and may not include a feedback process. It also does not always plan for evaluation in such an in-depth manner. Rather, change management methodology dictates the change that is needed and the outcome reported. It too connects the intervention to strategic goals if that is discussed at the information gathering stage. Kotter (1996) might assume that each step's successful implementation results from the successful accomplishment of the intervention, and that executives directly steer change. The assessment is planned and assessed by the leader with minimal outside input.

In contrast to the change management approach, the OD approach highlights the participation of organization members in the entire process. OD consultants play the role of facilitator to bring out participants' (clients') desired futures, while clients determine their own issues and actions of each step in a manner that is agreeable to all people involved in the change. Thus, assessing the status quo, making collaborative action plans, and assessing and taking responsibility for creating results (Rothwell et al. 2009) have something to do with the clients, not the OD consultants and executives. To sum up, including the aforementioned approaches, the steps in evaluation planning and the subsequent actions in an implementation step vary depending on their approaches but should be aligned and congruent with the principles and characteristics of their change approaches. Each approach has its merits, but when considering the importance of being able to show impact, the OD approach pulls in evaluation metrics at every step, making it flexible and adaptable.

4.5 Why Is Planning the Evaluation Critical in OD?

Evaluation refers to the process that assesses and demonstrates the value of what has been done, and it not only determines the financial values but also must consider nonfinancial worth (Rothwell & Sredl 2000). In this sense, an evaluation of OD provides an opportunity to demonstrate tangible outcomes of OD intervention as well as other factors such as customer and participant engagement, feelings, emotions, or interventions. Similarly, Porras and Berg (1978) argue that the impacts of OD intervention on an organization can be divided in two ways: individual and system outputs and human interactive process. The outputs of the individual and the system refer to the typical performance variables such as profits, costs, productivity, and efficiency, while the human interactive process variables include employees' behaviors, attitudes, and psychological characteristics such as openness to influence, trust, interaction, and motivation. Considering the wide variety of potential variables for an OD evaluation, the planning and determination of what has to be examined is a profound issue that should be determined from the start. If confusion or ambiguity in regard to goals and outcomes exists, those in charge of the OD event may draw improper conclusions and cannot ensure that their planned change will be accomplished. In the evaluation process, planning exactly what to evaluate and how to assess the OD intervention is critical.

4.6 Alignment of Goals to Evaluation

As seen in Figure 4.1, OD evaluation goals should be aligned with the OD problems and solutions in a seamless manner. OD problems and solutions are identified through needs assessment and the feedback process, providing

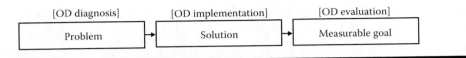

Figure 4.1 Alignment of the outcomes in the OD process.

the basis for measurable change goals. If OD consultants and clients improperly conduct the needs assessment in the diagnosis step and cannot identify the problems, this consequently results in choosing the wrong solutions and wrong evaluation objectives, resulting in failed change. Thus, in order to prevent this kind of mistake, OD consultants and clients should rigorously carry out a needs assessment before beginning any change effort including feedback activities that will allow for a linear linkage among these three factors, and if the first attempts at identifying a cause or issue is unclear, the assessment phase should continue so that the planning can be accurate.

4.7 When Is OD Evaluation Planning Conducted?

Early and often! It is a commonly held misconception that evaluation is a single event that is planned and implemented during the final step, after implementing change actions. On the contrary, it begins during the early planning stages and is expanded and revised in the early pre-execution or the contracting phases of OD intervention. However, OD evaluation should be implemented both during the intervention (formative) and after the intervention (summative).

Formative evaluation refers to the determination of whether the change intervention is going well and producing the intended outcomes. By identifying unexpected issues and obstacles of the change intervention, OD consultants can immediately take action on them to prevent rendering the interventions ineffective. Also, the data gathering and the feedback process for evaluation can serve as a communication vehicle during the intervention to ensure that participants are constantly engaged in individual change actions and to pay attention to team and organization-level actions.

Summative evaluation is immediately conducted after change to ensure that the change intervention offered values, merit, or worth on the levels of individuals, teams, or organizations. In this phase, OD consultants can also acquire knowledge and information as evidence that the change has been accomplished, supported, and sustained as intended as well as grasp participants' perceptions and feelings about change. This information can also be a basis of further decision making about an additional intervention strategy.

In fact, when the OD change is implemented as a long-term intervention or there is no exact ending date but rather a goal to reach a desired state, data gathering for evaluation in each stage can be an important index of whether further actions can proceed. Also, the data gathered and the feedback for action planning in each stage can be evaluation data to make further decisions. Given that OD evaluation is a part of the ongoing OD intervention, planning the evaluation strategy, including planning of the evaluation target, purpose, method, and timescale, should be rigorous and performed before implementing the change intervention.

This illustrates the central point of this chapter: evaluation planning is not the final step in OD intervention but one that is included in each stage of the process as it informs each next step and allows for adjustments and feedback from stakeholders along the way. This recursive practice decreases the possibility of missed information and misdirection, and therefore increases the overall success of the effort.

Despite the seemingly obvious importance of OD evaluation planning, it is rarely designed in the early stages and sometimes, without careful and deliberative planning, it is tacked on at the end as a matter of habit rather than purposeful execution. Why is the evaluation planning process overlooked or skipped? A predominant reason is that many clients regard evaluations as an optional step rather than as an essential part. Another possibility is that it is perceived to be too costly because of using too many resources, but what is really happening is that it was poorly planned, making it difficult to provide evidence of worth. The organization may worry about any negative impact of lackluster results, again possibly because of poor planning. Outside experts can assist in this area because they have the knowledge of evaluation and its importance to the change process and bring a new perspective to the situation.

4.8 Elements of the OD Evaluation Planning Step

The central purpose of OD evaluation planning is to clarify what to evaluate and remove any of the aforementioned causes that might impede the successful evaluation. The OD evaluation planning should be discussed early such as in the contracting phase in the OD process. In the OD contracting phase, OD consultants explore with clients their issues, problems, and needs and discuss how they will proceed with the change process. Multiple clients' or stakeholders' perspectives and needs can be different; OD consultants must help their clients to agree on the change objectives including the level of change intervention and the level of involvement from organization members. In this respect, in this phase, multiple stakeholders should agree on what the success of OD change should look like and what areas must be evaluated. The core tasks required of OD consultants are as follows.

4.8.1 Involve the Right People in the Evaluation Planning

To achieve successful OD evaluation, including designing an evaluation plan, carrying out the evaluation process, and reporting the results strategically, one of the essential tasks is to involve the right people in this evaluation process. People surrounding the OD intervention include the following:

- **Clients:** Clients are the people who participate in and are affected by OD intervention. Clients could be individuals, groups, intergroup, or organizations, depending on the level of interventions. Because of the size and complexity of change interventions, it is sometimes difficult to define exactly who the clients are. However, this is a fundamental question that should be defined and agreed upon because the whole process is largely affected by the clients.
- **Change Agent:** A change agent facilitates a change in the environment. A change agent "sets out to establish conditions and circumstances that are different from what they are now and then accomplishes that through some set or series of actions and interventions" (Ford & Ford, 1995, p. 543). Dunphy (1996) explains that the change agent roles can include (a) a technical expert who designs the change framework and intervention, (b) a social relationship facilitator who creates and promotes social interaction, and (c) a negotiator who reconciles diverse interests and needs of key parties.
- **Sponsor:** A sponsor is a person who is the main supporter of the change intervention. A sponsor can also be a change champion (being responsible for championing the change intervention), a change leader (influencing the success or failure of a change effort by executing the leadership for the change), and a change supporter (encouraging the front players in change intervention and offering cooperative assistance to accomplish the success of change). These multiple roles can be conducted by the same person and also more than one individual can play the same role together if it is more effective (Warrick 2009).

The following are the three individuals or groups that should be included in the OD evaluation planning: (a) who will plan the evaluation, (b) who will be evaluated (target group for evaluation), and (c) who will conduct the evaluation (in the next chapter, OD evaluator issues will be discussed). Before any of the details are worked out, it will be critical to ascertain who makes the decisions and represents the perspectives of the participants. This is not always easy as there can be competing ideas on the goals as well as the outcomes. A benefit to using an OD consultant is that they maintain an objective and balanced viewpoint, preventing a skewed plan or one that leaves out key viewpoints.

The OD consultant is often tasked with coordinating the entire change effort, which includes the evaluation, but they also can run a separate evaluation team apart from the change implementation team in order to reach an objective appraisal. In this case, a third party who takes charge of the evaluation planning should preserve their group's independence from the power in an organization. They will work with the organization to understand the objectives, how it connects with strategic goals, and what metrics are available, and to understand the stakeholders' group. Additionally, they will need access to appropriate resources that includes key people in the process.

4.8.2 Clarify the Evaluation Goals and Objectives

Another critical step in evaluation planning is to clearly determine specific evaluation goals and objectives. Clear evaluation goals and objectives should meet specific criteria. First, evaluation goals and objectives should align with the OD problems defined through the OD diagnosis phase. Next, ascertain client expectations and confirm that it is congruent with the evaluation goals and objectives. Once that is determined, then the identification of evaluation metrics becomes clear and successful evaluation is more likely to be achieved. Second, consider the specific needs of each stakeholder/stakeholder group and what specific metrics will be most effective in showing impact. Rather than determining the general area of evaluation, OD consultants and clients must include details about the level of evaluation. Finally, clarifying the evaluation goals and objectives means sharing and communicating with clients about the evaluation goals and objectives. It is important for change participants to share what their aims for change are, what the desired future state would look like, and how they can know their success to measure their accomplishments. By involving clients in the initial step, OD consultants can encourage them to be motivated for change and make them aware about what they are exactly

Table 4.1   Checklist for Starting Up the Evaluation Planning

Questions (Tasks to Be Done)	Check When Completed
What needs to be achieve through the OD intervention?	
What would the desired change state look like?	
What metric will be used to measure success for the desired change after the intervention?	
Who/which are the targets of change (e.g., people/group/units)? What level of change do we need?	
What are the specific evaluation expectations at each level?	
Are the evaluation expectations aligned with the aims and levels of the change intervention?	
Are you in agreement with each level of targets, with regard to evaluation goals and objectives?	

supposed to do. This shared information will also put the evaluation in better hands by leading clients actively participating in the data gathering process. Differences can be addressed and a congruent alignment should be achieved before starting the change efforts. Clients have ownership of OD change when they are actively involved in decision-making processes. To sum up, the questions in Table 4.1 can be raised in the evaluation planning step.

4.8.3 Develop the Evaluation Strategy

To perform the concrete evaluation process, it is essential to develop evaluation strategies that can guide the team as they carry out the evaluation process, events, and activities. The components of the evaluation strategy are varied and depend on the specific variables inherent in each organization. It will also vary in regard to how far the stakeholders are willing to be within their process. For instance, if the organization is undertaking a complex intervention with additionally complicated metrics, the OD consultants will invest considerable resources and energy to achieve a precise evaluation. If there are requests from key stakeholders and clients to simplify the evaluation process, you can plan simple evaluation steps by applying some of the metrics and methods that are the most appropriate for the analysis of an organization. However, assessing the impacts of the OD intervention indicates how successfully the OD consultants were and whether they performed their jobs and duties well based on the contracts; hence, evaluation is a very important metric for OD consultants as well. Caution is needed in this instance. If a simplistic or less than adequate evaluation is planned because of a lack of commitment (resources/time), then it could be deemed the fault of the consultant, not the process. Education is a role for the consultant, and accurate documentation is vital as a way of providing a historical perspective of the choices made along the way. Both planning and implementing the evaluation should be accurate and precise, whether it follows a comprehensive evaluation model or not.

Depending on the types of OD interventions and rigor used in creating high-quality evaluations, the design of evaluation models can be crafted in a variety of ways to assure that there is fit. According to Cady et al. (2009), when we decide how to develop the evaluation, there are two big themes that OD consultants should consider: Do key stakeholders and clients want to increase the rigor or do they want to limit resources?

Table 4.2 shows some important factors that might affect the decision on how extensive an evaluation to plan. Before developing evaluation strategies and tasks, OD consultants need to negotiate and make a clarification with key stakeholders and clients about the extent of the rigidity of the evaluation. Use this checklist to start a conversation with those in charge of the effort—it may bring underlying fears or misconceptions to light and could help clarify goals.

Then, what is the most practical way for OD consultants to plan the evaluation strategy before facing the evaluation phase? Figure 4.2 shows the practical guidelines for OD evaluation that OD consultants can use for the

Table 4.2 Influential Factors of Evaluation Strategy Planning

Demands for Evaluation	Resources for Evaluation
Accountability for results	Time for designing, data gathering, analyzing, and reporting
Deciding further investments	Time for employees participating in the evaluation
Revising the OD intervention strategy	Professionals from HR, finance, social research, and so on
Finding a success story	Consulting costs
Organization power and political situations	Opportunity costs (e.g., deferred decision)
Significance of results for employees' health and safety	Technology

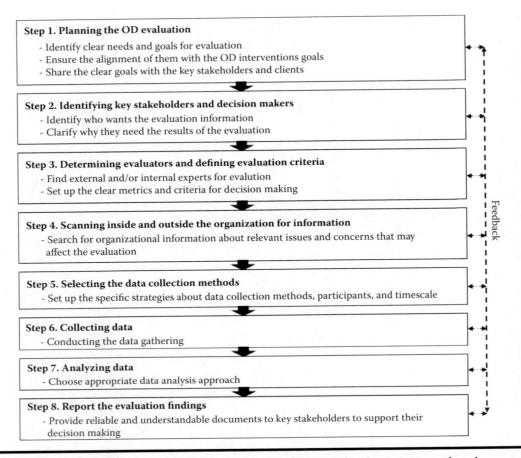

Figure 4.2   Eight-step practical guidelines for the OD evaluation strategy planning. (Adapted from Kim, W., Rashed, A., Park, C. H., & Rothwell, W. J. (2013). Practical guidelines and implications for organization development evaluation. In Chapman, D. D., & Desiderio, K. P. (Eds.), *2013 Conference Proceedings of the Academy of Human Resource Development*. St. Paul, MN: The Academy of Human Resource Development.)

evaluation process. These guidelines emphasize the importance of identifying key stakeholders and decision makers and the necessity of searching for the relevant organizational information and issues that affect or strain the evaluation results.

4.8.4 Agreeing on the Evaluation Planning with Key Stakeholders and Clients

It is important to reach an agreement with the client early in the change effort planning stages to prescribe what outcomes they hope to achieve. It is obvious that if there are unclear and blurred aspects in the process and methods, the evaluation results can raise doubts about the objectivity and fairness of the evaluation, making it unacceptable to clients. In fact, it is good practice to not move forward without a contract that outlines each criterion and expectation.

Finding common ground and purpose may be a challenge when there are a multitude of stakeholders involved who all have specific goals. It is also important for the key stakeholders and clients to have a sense of ownership of evaluation by participating in the evaluation decision-making process and agreement. Since they know well what kinds of assessment metrics exist in their organization, and what issues are underpinned by those assessment criteria, OD consultants can get ideas for the rigid OD evaluation. By sharing their information and ideas about evaluation metrics and methods, OD consultants can also develop advocates, who can provide support in the OD evaluation process. Given that key stakeholders and clients are key decision makers who pick up the action points from OD evaluation results and revise their OD strategy to make further actions, sharing all detailed information on evaluation planning is critical in the planning stage.

4.9 Chapter Summary

In summary, evaluation goals should be aligned with the identified OD issues and interventions because it increases the efficiency of the change process. OD consultants and participants in the planning phase should establish what the desired outcomes are as well as the metrics used to demonstrate success. Other vital decisions include the following: Who would be involved in the evaluation process? What matrix and methods would be employed? What timelines are proper based on the clients' expectations and the company's resources? The evaluation planning phase is the time to clarify these issues and make agreements among individuals who are involved in the OD program so that a congruent and aligned evaluation can complement the change effort.

References

Cady, S. H., Auger, J., & Foxon, M. (2009). Situational evaluation. In Rothwell, W. J., Stavros, J. M., Sullivan, R. L., & Sullivan, A. (Eds.), *Practicing Organization Development: A Guide for Leading Change*, 3rd ed., pp. 269–286. San Francisco, CA: Pfeiffer.

Dunphy, D. (1996). Organizational change in corporate settings. *Human Relations,* *49*(5), 541–552. doi:10.1177/001872679604900501

Ford, J. D., & Ford, L. W. (1995). The role of conversations in producing intentional change in organizations. *Academy of Management Review, 20*(3), 541–569. doi:10.5465/AMR.1995.9508080330

Kim, W., Rashed, A., Park, C. H., & Rothwell, W. J. (2013). Practical guidelines and implications for organization development evaluation. In Chapman, D. D., & Desiderio, K. P. (Eds.), *2013 Conference Proceedings of the Academy of Human Resource Development.* St. Paul, MN: The Academy of Human Resource Development.

Kotter, J. P. (1996). *Leading Change.* Boston, MA: Harvard Business Press. doi:10.1177/1534484305278283

Porras, J. I., & Berg, P. O. (1978). The impact of organization development. *Academy of Management Review, 3*(2), 249–266. doi:10.5465/AMR.1978.4294860

Rothwell, W. J., & Sredl, H. J. (2000). *The ASTD Reference Guide to Workplace Learning and Performance: Present and Future Roles and Competencies* (Volume II) (3rd ed.). Human Resource Development Press.

Rothwell, W. J., Stavros, J. M., & Sullivan, R. L. (2009). Organization development and change. In Rothwell, W. J., Stavros, J. M., Sullivan, R. L., & Sullivan, A. (Eds.), *Practicing Organization Development: A Guide for Leading Change,* 3rd ed., pp. 11–42. San Francisco, CA: Pfeiffer.

Warrick, D. D. (2009). Launch. In Rothwell, W. J., Stavros, J. M., Sullivan, R. L., & Sullivan, A. (Eds.), *Practicing Organization Development: A Guide for Leading Change,* 3rd ed., pp. 234–263. San Francisco, CA: Pfeiffer.

Chapter 5

Identifying and Examining Key Stakeholders/Decision Makers

Veronica David, Dara Sanoubane, and Maureen Connelly Jones

Contents

5.1 Introduction

A common complaint heard after any change is that employees were not included, not heard, not considered, or not communicated with along the way—left in the dark. When key stakeholders at any level feel excluded or forgotten, it can stand in the way of any effort to change direction or make improvements. Those on the outside might create obstacles or gather a coalition to oppose the formal plans. Therefore, it will be important to identify the stakeholders and decision makers, formal and informal, in the organization as early as possible.

5.2 Chapter Overview

This chapter will explain how executives, managers, employees, and consultants can identify key stakeholders and decision makers in an organization. Determining the key stakeholders in an organization is important to ensure that any type of change lasts. By utilizing the key concepts in this chapter, such as the tools, activities, key definitions, and theories, anyone can easily determine key stakeholders.

The following will be covered in greater detail:

■ Why stakeholders are important to the company/organization
■ Business case for including stakeholders in the evaluation process
■ What is stakeholder theory? And how can it be used to help the company?
■ How organizations can use various activities to work with stakeholders
■ Key definitions that can help determine stakeholders

5.3 Business Case Study

Introduction: In the past decade, a large, multicampus higher-education institution has been encouraged through its waste management and operations unit to reduce its waste production and decrease its overall energy consumption. Small programs and campaigns that encourage economically and environmentally sustainable practices in the classrooms and offices have been accepted *voluntarily.* The programs have enlisted behavior actions and changes identified as "low hanging" because they were considered easily attainable and required the least effort for the change agents. Examples would include turning off lights in a room when not in use, putting office computers to sleep mode when not in use, and placing plastic and paper waste in the recycle bin instead of the trash bin.

Background: After this 10-year period, an energy consumption assessment was conducted by the institution and found the following:

■ It employs 35,000 people who travel (collectively) 15 million miles by air and 7 million miles by road.
■ Among its campuses, the institution occupies and operates 1200 buildings.

- $40 million per year spent on goods and services with more than 500 suppliers.
- $20 million per year spent on the management of waste produced from the goods and services purchased for the institution.
- Through these current recycling programs and educational efforts toward sustainable practices, the institution has diverted approximately 7% of its recyclable and compostable materials from the landfill.

An institution-wide survey assessment indicated that there was a growing concern from the general student body, staff, and faculty regarding the institution's environmental impact and its lack of response and leadership to global warming issues. The president and university planning council responded by establishing a sustainability institute tasked with the mission of defining global warming and sustainability issues, and communicating and implementing strategic unit changes in response to these issues. Encouraging research and development regarding global issues would elevate the institution as a leader in this new and growing global issue.

Implementation: In support of this focus, the waste management and operations units have decided that a more thorough effort at waste management and more robust response to finding solutions to diverting compostable and/or recyclable materials from the landfill were needed. Additional efforts to reduce energy consumption and to lower overhead spending on materials, service, and general operations were a priority. An institution-wide waste diversion and reduction plan was created where individual trash bins in every office of every building of the institution's five campuses would be phased out and a common area to dispose of waste, composting, and recycling materials would be provided. Every one to two weeks, a building on campus was thoroughly converted to the new waste management system. Implementation of this change effort began 12 months earlier and full conversion completion is projected to take two years. A formative survey assessment of the implementation revealed positive feedback. However, some academic and student support service departments indicated significant dissatisfaction with the change.

Case Questions

1. Clearly the institution thought it was making a change—what steps do you think they missed? In what phases were they missed? What was the impact?

2. What stakeholders should have been included in the plan?
3. What is the impact of not identifying key players on the change process? The organization? The employee?

5.4 What Is "Stakeholder Theory?"

The first important clarification in this chapter is to define who is and who is not a stakeholder. Freeman (1984) suggested that a stakeholder is any group that "has a stake in or claim to the firm" (p. 39). This definition was a departure from the long-held belief that organizations focus solely on shareholders (those who own stock in a company). Freeman broadened who is considered important by including those who have a "moral claim" and "could benefit or be harmed by a corporation" (2002, p. 41). When trying to determine who stakeholders are within an organization, a struggle can ensue on how to begin. Gauging the importance of individuals within the organization can be difficult once you get beyond the obvious set of managers and executive team members. The main concern is that someone will be missed and another might be included that is not the right fit for the project. Because the process can be tricky, consultants and sponsors can utilize Freeman's (1984) Stakeholder Theory as a guide. The theory can be beneficial to help to determine not only who the important players are but also how to determine who they are.

5.5 Stakeholder Identification

Identifying the list of stakeholders should take careful thought and time should be set aside to gather ideas and sift through the list. To guide the creation of the list, stakeholder theory suggests that a "company should be run for the benefit of all those who may be deemed to have a stake in it and it identifies five categories of stakeholders: investors, employees, customers, suppliers, and the relevant community" (Argenti, 1997, p. 442). With that in mind, the consultant and organization should ask key internal players to develop their own list and then pool them to develop a central list. A guiding theoretical concept is that organizations should strategically manage their vision, mission, and operations to lean toward accountability, ethically do what is best for those it serves (Freeman, 1984). This should help the group to avoid restricting the options and consider all players who fit these criteria. To assist in identifying the right people and narrowing the list, use Tool 5.1. This tool will hopefully prevent the publishing of an incomplete list and avoid delays in the project.

In the evaluation and planning phases, the stakeholder identification becomes a highly focused process. The team needs to contemplate which stakeholders can provide input, guidance, information (data), networking, and expertise toward the development and implementation of the evaluation plan. This group of stakeholders may be unique as they will lend expertise to the evaluation (and maybe other phases) that might include data gathering, data mining, data base preparation, data visualization, customer service and vendor data, and more. Think broadly but purposefully for this group while following the general guidelines for stakeholder identification.

Once the group is defined, the important task of reaching out to each of them begins. Bringing them officially on board, answering questions, hearing ideas, and working to resolve any concerns is an important set of tasks. This outreach should be assigned to someone within the organization that has already connected and had the skill set to communicate as the face of the organization. This is a highly skilled role and should be assigned carefully as mishaps in this area may never heal and could negatively affect this project as well as future relationships.

Another group of folks that can lend focused support is the *secondary stakeholders*. This group often has an indirect interest in the goals of the organization or the change effort. Sometimes, someone in this group can overlap with a primary stakeholder. This group may have no financial interest and gain little from the organization but can be the most vocal, for instance, a local community service or environmental group.

So many benefits await from identifying the right group of people. The added perspective, input, and cooperation will be strategic in the implementation of the change effort. A communications specialist should be involved so that the messaging is crafted well and then a thoughtful communication procedure is implemented. Once the important individuals are identified, using the Stakeholder Theory, the change effort also should see a greater chance at a success rate—something any group would relish.

5.6 Challenges in Selecting Stakeholders

Stakeholder identification is difficult for some organizations and companies to address. For some managers, the burden of identifying their company's stakeholders may seem like an unconquerable challenge. It is a task dealt out with little education and direction, so often the list is incomplete or not on target for the planned project.

As a reminder, the selection should include key stakeholders such as investors, employees, suppliers, customers, and the community (Freeman, 1984) as key stakeholders. The challenges faced during this selection process may include the following:

- Misfit
- Overenthusiastic volunteers
- Hidden agendas
- Difficulty determining the main purpose of the stakeholder group (there may be more than one)
- Demonstrating the benefit of participation
- Prior lack of networking and inclusion of stakeholders
- Lack of participation

While the common impression is that only individuals are considered to be key players within an organization, Stakeholder Theory shows that anyone, and any group, who can be effected by the organization is a key player within that organization.

A seemingly simple and obvious task of any change effort is to identify the purpose, goals, and objectives. It seems that it would go without saying that the purpose should be clear, but often it is not, and more importantly, communication lacks. After everyone is on the same page, the discussion surrounding stakeholders can begin. A clear vision for the change effort will allow the selection of stakeholders who have direct connections with the issue, who can provide supportive information and advice, and who can clearly see how they can benefit from being included. Misfit will occur if project scope is unclear. It will be difficult to categorize stakeholders into suitable groups (those who fit the project, those who fit a particular part of the project, and those who are not a fit). The consulting team should work with leadership to communicate fully and often to keep the goal in mind for each member.

Hidden agendas should stay on the radar when evaluating possible stakeholders. This may occur when someone perceives benefit and works to get involved in order to realize a personal advantage. Many stakeholders may benefit from the efforts; however, conflict of interest and anything that is less than transparent should be scrutinized well. Stay objective and assess each person or group on its own merits. If they fit the project and there are no ethical or legal considerations to stand in the way, then bring them onboard in the appropriate capacity. If the fit lacks, then assure someone is tasked with communicating the rationale. Each organization is unique and its work can affect a wide array of community members. Some may come with a veiled plan while others are very up front with agendas; either way, make a standardized assessment. Keep an open door but maintain clear lines with the end goal in mind.

Upon identification of a company's key players, the next task is to identify the benefits and expectations that each of those players has related to their participation. Apart from the shareholders, who have a legal stake with a company, other stakeholders must be shown the benefits. Some may not enthusiastically embrace involvement in the project. During the initial conversations about the stakeholder group, the benefits and possible downsides to involvement should have been identified so that they can be clearly communicated. This then creates a burden on company managers to determine and delegate each key players' expectations and values. (Also, with such a great amount of power given to managers to play this role, abuse of such power may be of concern.) Now that the challenges are clear, let us look at some possible solutions.

5.7 Solutions to Stakeholder Concerns

It is clear that making all the right choices for inclusion in the stakeholder group may not be easy; however, it is a task that, with planning, can pull in the best people to support a successful evaluation and overall effort. With any project, multiple agendas can be in play. Here, again, it is critical that the purpose, goals, and objectives be clearly communicated often and to everyone involved. This allows team members to point to those directives when dealing with the challenging situations arising from hidden agendas, participation inconsistencies, and so on.

There are many different solutions that an organization can put in place to help address these challenges. An important item to note, while thinking about solutions, is that neglecting key players may be detrimental to the company as a whole. These issues were covered earlier in the chapter but bears repeating; deliberate contemplation is a must—broadening the list of possible stakeholders and allowing a variety of group members to suggest those to include should minimize the missed opportunity and subsequent bad feelings.

Perceived importance on the part of the stakeholder may also pose a challenge. While some individuals, or some groups, might feel that their role within or for the company is more important than it is, not taking their opinions into account is a bad practice to begin. All groups and individuals are important in their own way and deserve to be listened to. In fact, listening to their ideas could open up another avenue or give the group a new idea. Individuals or groups that do not need to be involved on a regular basis can be clustered in specialty groups and included on an "as needed" basis. Remember to include them in appropriate communication avenues.

The best way to look at solutions is to discuss the process of trying to identify key players within an organization. Company managers who need to identify stakeholders should work on revisiting and clarifying the change effort or, in some circumstances, the company's purpose. By doing so, they will be able to align the important players with the company's purpose. An example would be a company that states one of its purposes is to adhere to the markets for capital, labor, and goods and services. A company manager would use that to state that the key stakeholders would be investors, shareholders, employees, suppliers, and consumers. Depending on the company's mission and purpose, there could be other groups such as social and environmental lobbyists and private and public regulators who could be identified as stakeholders.

5.8 Communicating Expectations

Now that the stakeholders (and groups) have been defined, it will be imperative that individual and group expectations follow quickly. Chief among the priorities will be to delineate each set of expectations in writing so that messaging is consistent and readily available. In any project, especially an organization development (OD)–led one, elements will be revised along the way to better meet the needs of the change effort. If expectations change in response, then the communication plan needs to be activated to get the message to those involved. This may also necessitate a change in expectations. The importance of clear, consistent, and frequent communication cannot be underscored enough. Breakdown here will affect many areas of a project and is an unnecessary mistake if coordination of the stakeholders is given priority.

5.9 Chapter Summary

Upon establishing a clear purpose, goals, and objectives for the change effort and evaluation plan, determining critical stakeholders should follow relatively easily. In fact, many internal stakeholders may be involved in the project development and others added later. The next step is to identify expectations for each key stakeholders and stakeholder group. Sharing expectations keeps all members on the same page and allows the group to maintain focus. Challenges in selecting and working with the stakeholder group may arise and should be resolved right away—always refocusing on the purpose. Stakeholders can provide and receive benefit from inclusion in a change effort. It is up to the team to assure a smooth course.

Determining the key stakeholders in an organization is important to ensure that any type of change lasts. The different tools, activities, definitions, and theories provided in this chapter provide applicable methods to determine who the key stakeholders are for that organization and how to best communicate, support, and leverage stakeholders' needs toward goals that are desirable for all. Tool 5.1 helps the organization assess, identify, and determine legitimacy of its stakeholders. Tool 5.2 allows organizations to assess its social performance toward its identified stakeholders. Finally, Activity 5.1 provides a way to reflect and reassess stakeholder in order to gain a clearer, deeper, and perhaps new understanding of the perspectives of its key stakeholders. It is important for everyone involved in the change effort to understand whom the key stakeholders are in order to ensure that the effort is self-sustaining.

5.10 Key Definitions

Corporation: System of stakeholder groups, a complex set of relationships between and among interest groups with different rights, objectives, expectations, and responsibilities... survival and continuous success depend on the ability of its managers to create sufficient wealth, value, or satisfaction for those who belong to each stakeholder group, so that each group continues as a part of the stakeholder system (Clarkson, 1995, p. 107).

Legitimacy: (1) Referring to socially accepted and expected structures or behaviors, often is coupled implicitly with that of power when people attempt to evaluate the nature of relationships of society; (2) A desirable social good, that is something larger and more shared than a mere self-perception, and that it may be defined and negotiated differently are various levels of social organizations.

Marginal stakeholder: (1) For medium to large companies, these types of stakeholders are consumer interest groups, stockholders, and professional associations for employees; (2) They have a small stake in the company, so their potential threat to the company is very low, but they do have some type of stake in the outcome of the company making their opinion important (Savage et al., 1991, p. 66).

Mixed blessing stakeholder: (1) Plays a major role in any type of change an organization is trying to make by either becoming a strong supporter of the change or threaten the change efforts; (2) Usually consists of either employees who are essential to the organization, clients, or customers, and organizations with similar products or services (Savage et al., 1991, p. 67).

Nonsupportive stakeholder: (1) These types of stakeholders have the highest potential threat to a company and will cause the most distress to the organization's executives and managers; (2) Typically include competing organizations, labor unions, and the government (Savage et al., 1991, p. 66).

Power: (1) When a stakeholder shows influence over the organization; (2) Transitory, as it can be gained by a stakeholder as well as lost (Mitchell et al., 1997, p. 865).

Primary stakeholder group: One without whose continuing participation the corporation cannot survive as a going concern (Clarkson, 1995, p. 106).

Secondary stakeholder group: Those who influence or affect, or are influenced or affected by, the corporation, but they are not engaged in transactions with the corporation and are not essential for its survival (Clarkson, 1995, p. 107).

Stakeholder: Any group or individual who can affect or is affected by the achievement of the organizations objectives (Freeman, 1984, p. 46).

Supportive stakeholder (a.k.a. ideal stakeholder): The most wanted stakeholder by management and executives because they are the easiest to work with, and the type that will foster cooperation (Savage et al., 1991, p. 65).

Urgency: When a stakeholder needs immediate attention. Two conditions need to be met: (1) when a relationship or claim is of a time-sensitive nature, and (2) when that relationship or claim is important or critical to the stakeholder (Mitchell et al., 1997, p. 867).

5.11 Tools and Activities

Activity 5.1: Stakeholder Perspective Assessment

Directions:

1. Define your change effort purpose. Describe the goals and objectives.
2. Define the team that will provide input into the stakeholder group
3. Identify key stakeholders in this organization, using the Stakeholder Identification worksheet (Tool 5.1).
   - Primary stakeholder listing
   - Who will specifically connect with the evaluation planning and implementation team?
   - Are there any secondary stakeholders? If so list them and their specialty area.
4. Using the Stakeholder Identification worksheet (Tool 5.1), identify questions and data needed to assess the progress of the change effort.
5. How would your organization manage the change effort discussed in the case differently and why?

Purpose: To illustrate, identify, understand, and account for various needs of different stakeholder groups in the OD intervention and evaluation process.

Rationale: From a purely financial business perspective, there is empirical evidence that establishing strategic relationship with key stakeholders will have a direct influence on a corporation's financial performance. Developing relationships with stakeholders expands the organization's, and its leadership's, ability to understand and meet its mission. This increased awareness encourages a more holistic approach to the corporation's decision-making process and is a competitive advantage (Berman et al., 1999). Therefore, an effective stakeholder identification/understanding process and a stakeholder approach to decision making and evaluation will offer competitive edge for a corporation.

Tool 5.1: Stakeholder Identification

Purpose:

■ Defining who is considered to be a stakeholder can be difficult for anyone looking to implement a change initiative in a given organization.
By completing the chart below, and following the instructions, determining who the key stakeholders are can be decided easily.
■ Once the chart is complete, the names/positions with the highest total
are the more important stakeholders during that change effort being
implemented.

Directions:

1. Column 1: Write the name of each person who you believe to be a
stakeholder with his or her position/title and organization if an external
candidate.
2. Column 2: Identify the person within the organization that has a relationship with this stakeholder or who will be responsible for reaching
out to this stakeholder.
3. Columns 3, 4, and 5: Rank, using the scale below, the stakeholder on
power, legitimacy, and urgency (as defined at the end of the tool).
4. Column 6: Total all the numbers in the row and put the total in this last
column.
   – The stakeholder with the highest numbers are the most likely key
   players.
   – This is a highly unique process for each organization; therefore,
   there is no finite cut off for those who should be involved. Each
   person/group should be assessed based on this ranking and overall
   fit for the change effort.
   – Those with lower numbers need to be discussed further.

Scale:

1 = Does not apply to this person (group)
2 = Sometimes applies to this person (group)

3 = Often applies to this person (group)
4 = Frequently applies to this person (group)
5 = Always applies to this person (group)

Stakeholder Identification Tool					
Proposed Stakeholder: Name Position Organization	Organization Contact	Power (1–5)	Legitimacy (1–5)	Urgency (1–5)	Total

Tool 5.2: Visual Assessment of Stakeholder Agreeability to a Change Effort

Directions:

1. Identify a topic or issue of change for your organization and write it in the blank in section (A).
2. Create a list of key stakeholders and list each one in section (B).
3. Identify each stakeholder's possible reactions and perspectives in regard to the issue listed, and using a scale of 1–5, identify the scale of each stakeholder's level of agreeability to the change process. Check these levels in section (C).
4. Utilize the information and visual display to start a discussion on the positive and negative aspects of the change effort among various stakeholders and how to address these challenges.

(A) Change:						
(B) Stakeholders:						
(C) Agreeability:						
5						
4						
3						
2						
1						
Comments:						

Activity 5.2: Understanding the Perspectives of Various Stakeholders

Purpose: When an organization is in the process of new development, or in the process of starting a change effort, it is helpful to gain a clear understanding of the perspectives of its key stakeholders. Having a clear understanding of these perspectives will allow the organization to proceed with more awareness and understanding of possible consequences and reactions from various stakeholders. The tool below provides a method to internally examine the perspectives of various stakeholders within an organization when given a topic or issue of change. Use of this activity and tool is suggested for management teams in order to gather a quick visual display of upper and middle management's perception on the level of stakeholder agreeability to a change effort. The information gathered by this quick assessment can then be used as a discussion platform for maintain stakeholder involvement and for managing stakeholder reactions to a change effort.

Activity directions:

1. Review the case study provided in this chapter.
2. Use Tool 5.1 to identify the stakeholders in the case study.
3. Use Tool 5.2 to identify the different perspectives of these stakeholders in the given change effort.
4. In a small group, discuss the findings, challenges, and gains for each stakeholder.

Example for Activity 5.1 and Tool 5.2 (Using Chapter Case Study)

(A) Change:	Change in waste management system at a large research one higher education institution—eliminating individual office trash receptacles/implementing common spaces for recycling and waste					
(B) Stakeholders:	Student	Staff/faculty	Administration	Prospective students/ parents	Environment	Budget
(C) Agreeability:						
5					✓	
4	✓			✓		
3			✓			✓
2		✓				
1						
Comments:	+ Familiarity + Engagement with environmental issues − Requires education for behavior change	− Perhaps less familiar − Requires education for behavior change + Opportunity to lead in social change	+ Opportunity to provide leadership in social change among other similar institutions − Management of pushback	+ Positive image of institutional values	+ Reduction of waste into landfill	− Costs with initial start-up − Costs to maintain systems and education + Reduced fees at waste deliveries + Recyclable buybacks

References

Argenti, J. (1997). Stakeholders: The case against. *Long Range Planning, 30*(3), 442–445.

Berman, S. L., Wicks, A. C., Kotha, S., & Jones, T. M. (1999). Does stakeholder orientation matter? The relationship between stakeholder management models and firm financial performance. *Academy of Management Journal, 42*(5), 488–506.

Clarkson, M. E. (1995). A stakeholder framework for analyzing and evaluating corporate social performance. *Academy of Management Review, 20*(1), 92–117.

Freeman, R. E. (1984). *Strategic Management: A Stakeholder Approach.* Boston: Pitman.

Freeman, R. E. (2002). Stakeholder theory of the modern corporation. In Donaldson, T., & Werhane, P. (Eds.), *Ethical Issues in Business: A Philosophical Approach*, 7th ed., pp. 38–48. Englewood Cliffs, NJ: Prentice Hall.

Mitchell, R., Agle, B., & Wood, D. (1997). Toward a theory of stakeholder identification and salience: Defining the principle of who and what really counts. *Academy of Management Review. 22*(4), 853–886.

Savage, T., Nix, T., Whitehead, C., & Blair, J. (1991). Strategies for assessing organizational stakeholders. *Academy of Management, 5*(2), 61–75. Retrieved from http://www.jstor.org/stable/4165008

Chapter 6

Determining Evaluators and Evaluation Criteria

Jamal E. Al Khadhuri and Maureen Connelly Jones

Contents

6.1 Introduction

Organizations invest significant time and money into instituting a change effort and maintaining the effects. Organization development (OD) uses a comprehensive and systematic approach toward a successful change process or intervening approach (Golembiewski, 2002). However, the success of any change effort is often not fully realized because the team neglects to identify who will evaluate and by what criteria the change will be measured. Many emphasize the importance of evaluating OD or any change effort, but in reality, it is relegated to the end or forgotten altogether. This misstep leads to many issues, not the least of which is the financial impact. Unfortunately, the impact is often hidden or not overtly connected to the lack of evaluation planning—and the cycle continues.

6.2 Chapter Overview

Complexities in evaluating OD lie in determining evaluators and the criteria through which the OD process and its change effort will be measured against. The success of the evaluation plan depends on understanding every organization as a unique entity, and considers its different interdependent factors. Whether the OD approach used aims to focus on problem identification and implementation of an action plan or building on current strengths, incorporating an effective evaluation plan is key for the success of any change effort. This chapter will focus on criteria for identifying OD evaluators and in determining the best fit for evaluation criteria.

The chapter will cover the following areas:

- Key definitions of OD evaluation individuals/teams and evaluation criteria
- How to determine the evaluator
- Role of evaluators
- Determining the evaluation criteria, addressing the needs of stakeholders and decision makers, and who should determine the evaluation criteria
- Implications for the practice

6.3 Business Case Study

A wholesale organization that manages three branches has been experiencing plummeting sales for the last two years. In the last financial quarter, the organization reported decreased sales, as low as 25% when compared to the previous two years. The organization board requested a customer satisfaction and feedback survey to be done to investigate why sales have decreased dramatically.

The survey results indicated low customer satisfaction with the current customer services provided. The three branches also received low marks for management practices and slow response to customer needs.

The board decided to contract an OD consultant to identify the root cause(s) of the plummeting sales and reported customer dissatisfaction. After the creation of an OD team, the preliminary data were assessed and suggested that the main problem was rooted in employee disengagement. The data also indicated that there was a lack of employee communication from supervisors and management.

The organization board sent a message to the quality group that they wanted some way to *finally* show that the OD change effort worked, and that they were to take the lead in this effort. The quality management personnel had never done this big of an evaluation but knew they had to measure the interventions. They had some metrics based on their own success indicators created previously to report sales and business development data. That was the only conversation about evaluation during the effort, and at the 1-year mark, a report to the board was generated. After reading the report, the organization board members had more questions than answers and expressed their dissatisfaction with the results.

Case Questions

1. What is your assessment of the evaluation planning process? What was missed?
2. How would you approach the evaluation planning? Who would you have placed in charge of the process?
3. This team used preexisting sales metrics; was this the best choice? What metrics do you think could have been used to gather the best and most accurate data?

6.4 Selecting the Evaluator

What are the necessary skills to coordinate the evaluation plan for a change event? This can be a difficult task if the organization lacks an active data gathering and assessment team. An increasing number of organizations have met the current "big data" overload that is facing leaders today by adding analysts. However, few have crafted teams that truly understand what metrics measure the intended outcomes, what data need to be collected, and then how to utilize the data—it is not enough to have lots of it; there must be a plan and experts to lead the charge. This is no small task for any change effort, as had been said in previous chapters; the evaluation aspects are often minimized or left to the end. That mindset must change if there is going to be a substantial measurement of ongoing success and eventual impact. Evaluators and evaluation criteria should be part of the initial conversations and then play a part in every phase of the change effort.

6.5 Why Choose an OD Consultant or Practitioner?

Scholarly literature in the practice of OD evaluation is scarce; however, the intangible benefits of the OD change effort is well documented (Head & Sorensen, 2005). OD practitioners use a down-up approach to ensure the participation of different-level employees and ultimately have maximum employee buy-in of the change process. The OD down-up approach takes into account the fact that employees at all levels of the organization hierarchy are important when pursuing any development or change effort (Rothwell et al., 2010). Therefore, assessment of any issues, planning, implementation, and evaluation of the change effort should start with the lower-level employees because they know it best. The plans for the OD change effort and the level of employee involvement must gain senior leadership support to ensure its effective implementation and achievement of organizational goals (Rothwell et al., 2010).

Similarly, the OD evaluation process would be more effective when supported by management and more efforts are made to create employee buy-in for implementation. Determining the evaluator early in the planning phase of the change effort will lead to consistent implementation of the evaluation. This is an integral part of the OD effort because the evaluator, whether an individual or a group, will oversee or implement the evaluation process (Alzahmi et al., 2013) and serve as the translator to the board/executive committee.

6.6 Types of Evaluators

Using the OD systematic approach in the evaluation process entails the fundamental OD principle of allowing the client to decide how to plan and implement the evaluation of the change effort (Rothwell et al., 2010). However, this should be agreed upon in the planning phase of the OD process as the OD consultant shares information, provides feedback, and explores the appropriate assessment and evaluation metric options. The evaluators of the OD change effort are divided into two types:

1. Internal evaluators
2. External evaluators

The decision on which type of evaluators and evaluation process to use is based on the resources and the proposed OD interventions. Alzahmi et al. (2013) suggest that some of the resources involved are the human, financial, or technical needs associated with implementation. These factors may influence whether an internal or external evaluator (or combination of both) is chosen. Let us look at the three options.

Internal evaluators are from within the organization and are usually members or indirectly involved in the main OD change effort team. The evaluator(s) must be knowledgeable regarding the change effort about to happen and, more important, possess the competencies to be an evaluator, which will be discussed in the next section. The benefits of an internal evaluator include having historical perspective, an understanding of how the organization functions, knowledge of the key stakeholders, and as such they need little orientation time to get up to speed with the change effort. However, being an insider is not always the best option. Working from the inside means that the evaluator(s) may have too much history with the organization, may be too conformable with the status quo, may not have organizational influence (may not be seen as a leader), or may be chosen for their seniority but lack the necessary competencies. When focusing on accountability the best choice is an evaluator from the outside as it helps to decrease conflict of interest issues. However, if independence is not of importance and the evaluation ensures that the change effort succeeded in accomplishing its goals and stakeholder expectations, then the evaluation process could be conducted through internal evaluators. The internal evaluators take the form of a participatory effort such as evaluation taskforce teams or as part of the human resources (HR) or quality management departments.

Another option would be for the organization to hire an **external evaluator** that has the requisite competencies and skill sets to coordinate the OD process and evaluation plan. An outsider provides the organization with multiple benefits that will help them achieve the stated goals. An outsider is free from any prior failures, morale issues, tension between departments or leaders, and comes to the effort with a blank slate. Many consultants will avoid hearing about prior issues so that they do not create any preconceived biases. A fresh set of eyes can also help the group see new possibilities and be open to novel interventions and, in the evaluation arena, be open to the resources needed to execute the plan. The downside is similar to the upside owned by an internal candidate in that the consultant will need to learn about the organization; become familiar with the issues, procedures, and resources; and gain trust.

The leadership team has another option—a **hybrid** where they use both an internal member and hire a consultant. This may be the best of both worlds. Choosing evaluators that complement each other's skill sets may allow for the most efficient and accomplished process when determining metrics, assessing data, and then reporting out findings. If there is a lack of expertise in any of the evaluative areas, this option allows the organization to carefully choose a consultant that can bring capability to the event. The internal employee can support the consultant by familiarizing him or her with procedures, access to resources, and inclusion in meetings.

The choice of evaluator, like with each phase of a change process, must be tailored to meet the needs of the organization and the solutions they are trying to implement. The decision requires a self-assessment of the leadership team and culture in an effort to analyze which of the options will benefit them the most. Access to the team and resources must be a commitment the principals take seriously for whomever is chosen.

6.7 Evaluator Competencies

A consideration that must occur in conjunction with the evaluator choice is a competency conversation on two levels: which competencies does the project need and which evaluators meet those criteria. "*Competencies*, then, are characteristics that individuals have and use in appropriate, consistent ways in order to achieve desired performance. These characteristics include knowledge, skills, aspects of self-image, social motives, traits, thought patterns, mind-sets, and ways of thinking, feeling, and acting" (Dubois et al., 2004, p. 11).

With this definition in mind, some organizations may not feel qualified to make this important, initial decision. They can still make a good decision by consulting a group or individual that does OD. They can be helpful in assessing the situation and creating the listing of competencies the group can move forward with as they select. If things go well, the consultant(s) may continue and be hired on as part of the team. An evaluator must be able to do two things: make evaluation decisions and then implement the evaluation plan (King et al., 2001). This is broad in scope and requires a further dive into specifics.

OD practitioners are uniquely positioned for this task as they use a participatory process to facilitate change efforts within an organization by guiding employees and their managers in making more effective decisions. Similarly, the evaluation process of OD interventions uses a participatory approach to determine the different areas and levels to be evaluated. These levels may be reflected in a formative, summative, or combined format, and they are applicable when using the action research (AR) model (evaluation phase) or the appreciative inquiry model (design and destiny phase).

Therefore, as guide for identifying OD evaluators, the evaluator competencies will be discussed concisely. King et al. (2001) proposed a set of evaluator competencies. However, in a follow-up study, King and Stevahn (n.d.) concluded that an evaluator should have, at a minimum, the following six competencies (specifics listed under each one). This list can be used as a basis for a checklist, modifying as needed:

1. Professional practice
   a. Applies evaluation standards
   b. Works ethically
   c. Respects all stakeholders
   d. Considers the general and public welfare
   e. Contributes to the knowledge base
2. Systematic inquiry
   a. Understands knowledge base
   b. Knows quantitative and qualitative methods
   c. Knows mixed methods
   d. Conducts literature reviews
   e. Specifies program theory
   f. Frames evaluation questions
   g. Designs the evaluation and collects and interprets data
   h. Makes judgments and recommendations
   i. Provides rationales for decisions

     j. Reports procedures and results

     k. Notes evaluation strengths and limitations

     l. Conducts meta-evaluations

3. Situational analysis

     a. Describes program

     b. Determines program evaluability

     c. Identifies stakeholders' interests

     d. Serves intended users' informational needs

     e. Addresses conflicts

     f. Attends to evaluation use

     g. Examines organizational and political context

     h. Attends to organizational change

     i. Respects site and client uniqueness

     j. Remains open to input

     k. Modifies evaluation as needed

4. Project management

     a. Responds to request for proposals RFPs

     b. Negotiates with clients

     c. Writes formal agreements

     d. Communicates with clients

     e. Budgets evaluation

     f. Justifies cost

     g. Identifies needed resources

     h. Uses technology as appropriate

     i. Supervises and trains others

     j. Conducts evaluation in a nondisruptive manner

     k. Presents work in a timely manner

5. Reflective practice

     a. Knows self

     b. Reflects on practice

     c. Pursues professional development in both evaluation and content areas

     d. Builds professional relationships

6. Interpersonal competence

     a. Uses written and verbal/listening communication skills

     b. Uses negotiation skills

     c. Uses conflict resolution skills

     d. Facilitates constructive interpersonal interaction

     e. Demonstrates cross-cultural competence (King & Stevahn, n.d.)

Stevahn et al. (2005) proposed that competencies are so important because there is no recognized licensure or credentialing for program evaluators. However, many OD practitioners have credentials in HR management or other additional education that demonstrate competence in the change process and specifically evaluation.

The **profession practice competency** denotes that the practitioner hold to ethical and industry standards. The **systematic inquiry** competency refers to the ability of the evaluator to practice research activities, implement evaluation-oriented activities, design tools, collect data, and interpret data for research and evaluation. **Situational analysis** calls for the evaluator to survey the big-picture issues in the organization and use that information to craft a company-specific plan while remaining open to ideas. **Project management skills** are the next "must have" competency. **Practicing reflectively** is the fifth competency area and brings attention to the evaluator's ability to self-assess and maintain current education in this arena. The last competency, **interpersonal competence**, focuses on "people skills" including conflict management and negotiation. This is just one model for assessing the competency of the evaluator, internal or external. It does provide a framework that shows the intricacy of this role and the specificity of the skills needed to do the best job. Now, let us move onto a conversation about the role of the evaluator.

6.8 The Roles of Evaluators

The roles of the evaluator(s) are determined at the initial planning steps of the OD effort to ensure effective implementation and organization-wide buy-in to the evaluation process. As every company is unique, so is every change effort. The following section looks at the broad scope for this role, knowing that more specificity is needed and should occur in the initial phase of the project. Advocacy, information gatherer, analyzer of metrics, and communicator are the general roles. The evaluator will serve as an advocate for an intertwined, consistent, and evidenced measurement for each goal set forth by the team. In this role, they will assure that evaluation takes a prominent place in the meetings and planning. They advocate for evidence, not people or departments, so staying objective and true to the goals is key.

Another integral role is to gather as much information as possible from as many sources to ensure that the correct data are being gathered and analyzed so that they may support demonstrating the effectiveness of the interventions. During data gathering, they should be given access to anyone who can augment information on where data are collected, existing data collection tools, the need to build new tools, and databases. Decisions should be made with the end in mind but also take into consideration information gained in the "feedback loop." If information is not funneled to them, they will seek it out.

Metrics are the cornerstone of the evaluation plan and the evaluators will suggest what they deem the most efficient and effective way to show merit in the change effort. Possible metrics are discussed later in the chapter. Often this is the most daunting task in any project owing to the volume of information and the dispersed nature of the data. Most departments are unaware of the type of data that are being collected elsewhere in the company. The best practice is to have an information guru that understands the kind of data needed and who and where it is being collected. The evaluator should be able to avoid duplication and streamline the activity of measurement.

The final broad role is as communicator. Communication specific to evaluation is key and keeps all the stakeholders in the loop. This role is specified in the overall planning meetings as well and may be focused on funneling information to the CEO and then they disseminate. Whatever direction the communication path takes, the emphasis is on maintaining open transmission lines. Again, this can help avoid duplication, catch potential problems early, keep stakeholders up to date, and provide an avenue for the members to share what is working and what may need to be adjusted.

Another area that should be taken on, in part, by the evaluator is that of demonstrating return on investment (ROI). In their 2013 book, Phillips et al. (2013) highlight the importance of including an ROI philosphy when evaluating the effectiveness of OD interventions. This section will concentrate on the immediate need to demonstrate ROI with each intervention and change effort. They explained that in order to implement and sustain an effective evaluation effort that validates ROI, roles are clearly delineated for the evaluators (Phillips et al., 2013). The evaluation roles include the following:

1. Evaluation champion
2. Evaluation leader
3. Member of an evaluation taskforce (Phillips et al., 2013)

The evaluation champion is an individual who supports the evaluation process and has skills in implementing the ROI method. This person is willing to sponsor the evaluation effort and teach others to ensure its succesful implementation. The leader could be one person or a team established to lead the evaluation process. This person is skilled in the evaluation methodology and is capable in managing the different levels of the OD change effort. Organizations may form an evaluation taskforce to implement and manage the details of the evaluation process. The member of the taskforce should be involved in the OD change effort and should work toward achieving the identified evaluation process goals, and their roles and responsibilities should be developed by the main OD team early in the process (Phillips et al., 2013).

Everyone performs better when their role is clear and that is no different in this role. Communicating this role to everyone involved will avoid confusion and misinterpretation as every role is ctitical to the success of a project. After the role becomes clear, the evaluator needs to get on to the main tasks at hand, determining metrics. The next section begins that discussion.

6.9 Determining the Evaluation Criteria

The traditional Action Research Model is one of the models used to guide a systematic OD process, and comprises eight steps: entry, start-up, assessment and feedback, action planning, intervention, evaluation, adoption, and separation (Cady & Caster, 2000; Porras and Berg, 1978). The comprehensive nature of the OD practice using the AR model or others reflects the importance of using an evidence-based methodology when implementing a change process. Consequently, the ideal approach to implementing an evaluation process is by integrating it throughout the OD change effort.

According to Nicholas (1979), the evaluation criteria should not focus on whether a program is effective or not, but more on the achievement of the goals set. This means that the evaluation criteria should be determined or developed based on the preintervention state and then the resulting situation after the implementation of the OD interventions. This will ensure that the evaluation method will measure the variables specifically pertaining to the idenified problems and interventions used and minimize the effect of the irrelavant variables on the outcomes of the evaluation (Nicholas, 1979).

Each project will have its own needs but there are some main categories of metrics that can be used. Some of the measurement categories would include the following:

- Compliance (against a standard—internal or external)
- Impact (net effect), outcome (outputs and outcomes)
- Process (new business processes, improvement)
- Workload (resource requirements, number of people needed, transactions, etc.)
- Risk (risk reduction or elimination)

Metrics can be divided into short-term, mid-term, long-term, and definitive time frames (National Institue of Environmental Health Services, 2014). This can be helpful when determining if the project has the correct incremental evaluations that meet the overall goals. Create a spreadsheet that has a column for each time frame (you may want to leave definitive out as it is uncommon) and list each of the metrics you choose in the column that fits the time frame best. For example, if there are no long-term metrics, then that should spark a conversation to pinpoint a miss or agree that there are no long-term goals. The following is a list of possible metric categories; this is in no way an exhaustive list but instead should be used as a brainstroming starter exercise.

- Audit reports
- Behavior change
- Sales numbers
- Recrutiment and retention numbers
- On-boarding costs, retraining costs
- Efficiency
- Capacity
- Sustainability
- Productivity
- Research funding

6.10 Who Should Determine the Evaluation Criteria?

Since there are no set criteria for the OD evaluation process owing to the unique nature of every situation and organization, the stakeholders, including members of the OD team, are in the best position to determine the evaluation criteria (Bryson et al., 2011). The OD practitioner may guide the process of identifying the evaluation criteria when contracted to do so. The OD practitioner will continually feed back information he or she hears/gathers to the team so that they may make the best decisions possible. This unique approach of the OD field makes having standard evaluation criteria unsustainable and as reported in the literature may lead to invalid outcomes (Bryson et al., 2011; Nicholas, 1979).

6.11 Addressing the Needs of Stakeholders and Decision Makers in Evaluation

Another important component that should be considered while determining the evaluation criteria is to identify the target audience for the outcomes of the evaluation process. Organizations may invest a lot money and time into the development and implementation of an evaluation process, and end up benefiting from a fraction of the comprehensive results generated. Therefore, it would be more cost-effective if the stakeholders and decision makers participate in identifying the key criteria for evaluating the OD interventions (Alzahmi et al., 2013; Nicholas, 1979).

Here are four questions to guide the choice of evaluation criteria and maximize the stakeholder buy-in. Building on the work of Alzahmi et al. (2013), the following questions will be discussed:

1. **Which content or predetermined problems should be addressed by the evaluation criteria?**

   The OD evaluation approach should focus on the issues and the problems identified through the participatory process created by the OD practitioner. Therefore, the content addressed by the evaluation criteria should reflect the identified problems and the OD interventions used to address these problems.

2. **What stakeholders have interest in the outcomes of the OD evaluation?**

   Every organization has its unique OD needs and share of problems that affect its employees' performance and productivity. These needs and problems will depend on the industry, the size of the organization, the influence of the (global) market, and the diversity of services and products rendered. Therefore, the stakeholders' interest will pivot on the organization and the OD change effort undertaken. Some examples of stakeholders and decision makers who have interest in the evaluation outcomes include senior management, HR units, managers, customers, or the general employee population.

3. **Why do the stakeholders and senior management need evaluation outcomes?**

    Once the stakeholders or the senior management have been identified, the OD evaluator should discover what information is critical to each group/individual. Confirming expectations and needed data will create a more impactful report of findings for each group and increase the overall value of the evaluation process.

4. **When do the stakeholder and senior management need the evaluation outcomes?**

    A final important area is determining the timeline for reporting results. Isolating key time frames from each stakeholder again increases the value of the process and provides support to each group (easily demonstrating the benefits of being involved in the project). This will also allow the evaluator to develop or adapt the evaluation tool at different times and according to the stakeholders' needs and input.

6.12 Implications for the Practice of OD Evaluation

Determining evaluator and evaluation criteria is an important component of OD evaluation and poses different implications for the practice OD and the individuals evaluating such effort. The challenge lies on understanding the nature and complexities of the OD process to manage a successful OD evaluation. Therefore, evaluators should be well versed in the practice of OD and the process used to accomplish its results. OD requires long-term commitment and that must be reflected in determining its evaluation criteria, methodology used, and the time and type of outcomes reported (Morrison, 1978). The alignment of the evaluation with the different steps of the change effort ensures a flow of continuous feedback and could help the OD practitioner and the decision makers improve the implementation of the change.

6.13 Chapter Summary

OD practitioners should develop the necessary evaluation competencies to create and implement an evaluation plan. Among those competencies, the evaluator needs to be able to determine the metrics essential to measuring the identified outcomes. Stakeholder involvement and using a participatory approach when developing the evaluation criteria will yield to a more systematic implementation and organizational buy-in.

6.14 Key Definitions

Evaluation criteria: Since there was no specific and uniform definition for the concept of OD evaluation criteria, the term will be used in this chapter to reflect the key steps or initiatives that reflect the identified problem and the OD intervention developed.

Evaluator: It is the individual leading the OD evaluation process, and the members of the evaluation taskforce external from or within the organization (Dunlap, 2008; Phillips et al., 2013).

OD intervention: It is a change effort or process that an organization or a system undergoes, and which is introduced by a change agent. It is the practical application of a planned change using evidence gathered from the organization and its employees (Cummings & Worley, 2014; Rothwell et al., 2010).

Organization effectiveness: It is the extent to which an organization performs and achieves its goals and strategies (Phillips et al., 2013).

6.15 Tools and Activities

Activity 6.1

Directions: Identify an OD change effort that your organization is undergoing or has gone through in the past. Complete the following activity worksheet by specifying eight examples of OD evaluation criteria and the place or person where the identified criteria could be validated. This activity is intended for OD practitioners and change effort leaders to assist in compiling a list of criteria for the OD change effort and where or by whom these criteria would be best validated. Note: Ensuring validity in this activity refers to confirming if the needs of the person, place, or team identified have been met or not.

Change Effort:		
Sr. #	*Example of OD Evaluation Criteria*	*Place/Person to Validate Criteria Relevance*
1.		
2.		
3.		
4.		
5.		
6.		
7.		
8.		

Activity 6.2

Based on the reading from this chapter and your own experience, identify three general advantages and three disadvantages of choosing an external evaluator compared to an internal evaluator to conduct the OD evaluation by completing the following worksheet activity.

Type of Evaluator	Advantages		Disadvantages	
External Evaluator	1.		1.	
	2.		2.	
	3.		3.	
Internal Evaluator	1.		1.	
	2.		2.	
	3.		3.	

	Tool Form 6.1:		
	Determining the Organization Development Evaluator—A Decision-Making Guide		

Instructions: List the different challenges to the different determinants or guiding questions on the left column, and check the column on the right for any completed evaluator determinants.

Sr. #	Evaluator Determinants	Challenges	Check All That Apply
1.	Is an external or an internal evaluator going to be used?		
2.	Has the cost of contracting an external evaluator been determined?		
3.	Is the external evaluator going to be the contracted OD consultant?		
4.	If the external evaluator is going to be different from the OD consultant, do you know someone who fulfills the required evaluator competencies? *Refer to the competencies identified in this chapter.		
5.	If using an internal evaluator, is it going to be one individual or will a taskforce be developed?		
6.	Is the evaluator going to report to or be part of a specific department in the organization? (e.g., HRD, quality management, planning, etc.)		
7.	Is the evaluator going to be a member of the central OD change effort team?		
8.	Does the specified evaluator have senior management support?		
9.	Is it cost-effective for the organization to release this individual from his or her main responsibilities to assume the internal evaluator role?		
10.	Is a specific member of senior management identified for the evaluator to report to and seek guidance when necessary?		

Concluding comments:

_____

_____

_____

_____

	Tool Form 6.2: *Organization Development Evaluation Criteria Guidelines' Checklist—Gathering Preliminary Data*

	Instructions: Place a check on the left column for all the areas accomplished to guide you in determining the OD evaluation criteria (to be completed by evaluator).
	Questions/Statements for Consideration
	1. Have you had a preliminary meeting with different stakeholders regarding determining the evaluation criteria?
	2. Is senior management in support of determining evaluation criteria and initiating an evaluation process?
	3. Have the stakeholders and/or the senior management given feedback about what outcomes they expect from the OD evaluation?
	4. Have the stakeholders and/or senior management given feedback how the results of the OD evaluation will be used in the future?
	5. Has the required format of the evaluation outcomes been identified?
	6. Has a specific time period been identified for providing a summary of feedback and results based on the required format established?
	7. Is there a consensus among the stakeholders and senior management on who would have access to the outcomes of the OD evaluation?
	8. Are the criteria focused on the identified problem and the OD interventions, rather than on the effectiveness of the overall OD effort? (to ensure validity and evaluation of different levels of the OD process)
	9. Are the evaluation criteria in alignment with the goal and the OD process?

References

Alzahmi, R. A., Rothwell, W. J., & Kim, W. (2013). A practical evaluation approach for OD interventions. *International Journal of Research in Management, Economics and Commerce, 3*(3), 43–65. Retrieved from http://indusedu.org/IJRMEC/March2013(Pdf)/4.pdf

Bryson, J. M., Patton, M. Q., & Bowman, R. A. (2011). Working with evaluation stakeholders: A rationale, step-wise approach and toolkit. *Evaluation and Program Planning, 34*(1), 1–12. doi:10.1016/j.evalprogplan.2010.07.001

Cady, S. H., & Caster, M. A. (2000). A diet for action research: An integrated problem & appreciative focused approach to organization development. *Organization Development Journal, 18*(4), 79–94.

Cummings, T., & Worley, C. (2014). *Organization Development and Change.* Mason, OH: South-Western Cengage Learning.

Dubois, D. D., Rothwell, W. J., King-Stern, D. J., & Kemp, L. K. (2004). *Competency-Based Human Resource Management.* London: Quercus.

Dunlap, C. A. (2008). Effective evaluation through appreciative inquiry. *Performance Improvement, 47*(2), 23–29. doi:10.1002/pfi.181

Golembiewski, R. T. (Ed.) (2002). *Ironies in Organizational Development Second Edition, Revised and Expanded,* 2nd ed., pp. 1–668. New York: Marcel Dekker Inc.

Head, T. C., & Sorensen, P. F., Jr. (2005). The evaluation of organization development interventions: An empirical study. *Organization Development Journal, 23*(1), 40–55. Retrieved from http://search.proquest.com/docview/197994838?accountid=13158

King, J. A., Stevahn, L., Ghere, G., & Minnema, J. (2001). Toward a taxonomy of essential evaluator. *American Journal of Evaluation, 22*(2), 229–247. doi:10.1177/109821400102200206

King, J. A., & Stevahn, L. (n.d.). Essential competencies for program evaluators (PowerPoint slides). Retrieved from: http://www.cehd.umn.edu/OLPD/MESI/spring/2015/KingStevahn-EssentialCompetencies.pdf

Morrison, P. (1978). Evaluation in OD: A review and an assessment. *Group & Organization Management, 3*(1), 42–70. doi:10.1177/105960117800300010

National Institute of Environmental Health Services (2014). Evaluation Metrics: Partnerships for environmental public health. Retrieved from: https://www.niehs.nih.gov/research/supported/assets/docs/j_q/peph_evaluation_metrics_manual_chapter_7_508.pdf

Nicholas, J. M. (1979). Evaluation research in organizational change interventions: Considerations and some suggestions. *The Journal of Applied Behavioral Science, 15*(1), 23–40. doi:10.1177/002188637901500104

Phillips, P. P., Phillips, J. J., & Zuniga, L. (2013). *Measuring the Success of Organization Development.* American Society for Training and Development. VA: Alexandria, ASTD Press.

Porras, J. I., & Berg, P. O. (1978). Evaluation methodology in organization development: An analysis and critique. *The Journal of Applied Behavioral Science, 14*(2), 151–173. doi:10.1177/002188637801400202

Rothwell, W. J., Stavros, J. M., Sullivan, R. L., & Sullivan, A. (Eds.). (2010). *Practicing Organization Development: A Guide for Leading Change.* San Francisco, CA: John Wiley & Sons.

Stevahn, L., King, J. A., Ghere, G., & Minnema, J. (2005). Establishing essential competencies for program evaluators. *American Journal of Evaluation, 26*(1), 43–59. doi:10.1177/1098214004273180

Chapter 7

Organization Development/ Change and Evaluation: External and Internal Sources to Consider

Edwin Mouriño

Contents

7.1 Introduction: Background and Driving Forces

In order to effectively evaluate organization development (OD)/change efforts, information needs to be gathered and analyzed from both external and internal sources. Organizations find that they have to change primarily because of the need to thrive and reinvent themselves while existing in a volatile, uncertain, complex, and ambiguous (VUCA) global competitive environment (Berinato 2014).

Despite many organizational changes, numerous books, and articles, as well as research papers written on the topic of organizational change, there are still many organizations that have failed in their organizational change efforts. One reason might be that while there are many OD projects taking place, very few are fully evaluated (Koivisto et al. 2008). Another reason might be that employees may not understand or like the change and in turn resist it (Maurer 2010), or because there is a lack of communications about the change effort (Kotter 2007). Finally, yet importantly, the leadership team has probably not collectively considered both external and internal sources in their evaluation efforts in order to have a comprehensive view of their change effort, possibly leaving important voices out.

7.2 Chapter Overview

This chapter will focus on and address both the external and internal sources that an organization, their leadership, and their OD/human resources (HR) practitioner or consultant should consider when considering what internal and external sources of information are needed in the evaluation strategy. The chapter will provide the following:

- Rationale for why external and internal resources need to be considered when evaluating an OD/change effort
- A case study with questions to reflect on when considering external and internal resources for evaluation of the potential OD/change effort
- Organizational trends that are causing organizations to change with external and internal sources/resources to consider
- Key takeaways
- Tools/checklists to consider when exploring external and internal sources when devising an evaluation strategy in order to address an OD/change effort

This chapter looks to address and focus on both external and internal sources and resources to consider when developing an evaluation strategy for the organization's OD/change effort. This will be done by highlighting an example of some of the human capital trends that are presently taking place and causing leadership to reassess how to prepare their organizations for the future of work and how to lead their organizations through needed changes as organizations are faced with a VUCA (volatility, uncertainty, complexity, and ambiguity) environment. Second, this chapter will address the sources to consider both from an external and internal perspective when looking to develop an evaluation strategy for their respective organizational change and development project(s). Next, the chapter will highlight a couple of checklists, a series of questions, and considerations that can be used as part of the evaluation strategy regarding external and internal sources/resources when organizations, their leadership, and their OD/change practitioners embark on an organizational change project.

The chapter will include a case study as an example that the reader can use to reflect, analyze, and consider, including questions on both external and internal sources on how to tackle the situation from an OD/change evaluation perspective.

Last, the chapter will summarize what has been addressed in the chapter along with closing thoughts to consider.

7.3 Business Case

The following case study looks at an organizational request for change and addresses areas to keep in mind both externally and internally as the case, organizational need, and client request take place.

Your objective—to assess the present situation and assess what external and internal sources to consider for this OD/change potential intervention with this client regarding her request.

A vice president (VP) client calls rather frustrated that her organization is requesting (really demanding) that you set up customer service training for her organization. She is the executive responsible for the Financial Services. She is based in the northeast and her Financial Services Division (250 employees) organization is based in the south. They provide financial support such as employee payroll, expense accounts, budgeting, and so on for the entire enterprise.

When she first took over the division (a couple of months ago), she toured the larger enterprise (that her organization supports), visiting her executive clients to assess their satisfaction (or lack of it) with her division. She got an earful from them on their lack of satisfaction on many levels. Just today, she tried to call her division for more than 3 hours and could not reach anyone by phone. This was the last straw and caused her to call you. She wants you to help her in delivering customer service training for the organization in order to improve their customer service. However, you have heard that there has been customer service training over the last few years with the organization and you being a good consultant, believe you need to know more.

With this information and understanding her frustration, you know that you cannot jump right in and create a plan until you have more details. You need to address her concerns, but before running off with her request, you have asked to speak to her direct management staff to get their perspective. She has agreed and now you need to gather as much data as possible, but how to go about it is the question. What next and what external and internal sources should be part of your data gathering strategy?

The following are some sources and questions to consider:

External considerations:
1. What are some external sources (best practices, benchmark information) you should consider as you develop a plan to address her request?
2. What are the market factors (competition of like organizations) that may affect the situation?
3. What experts should you be speaking with outside of the organization?
4. What clients should you engage to gather data?

Internal considerations:
1. You will need to design questions to ask your client—what do you need to understand to begin? What can they tell you about the culture, people, and business practices?
2. Whom should you speak with internally in addition to her management team?
3. What questions should you be asking her management team? What of morale, leadership style, openness to change/questions/ideas, teamwork, and others should be considered?
4. Are there instruments, surveys, or other resources you should consider? Using a validated (research evidence that it measures what

it says it measures) tool is very important so that it does what you need it to and it helps validate the information gathered, making it more credible.

5. What organizational metrics should you review? What data exist that could help shed light on the root cause of their issues?
6. What is your client's end goal? Leadership's goal(s)?

This case exemplifies the typical introduction to a client and the stated problem. The case and questions are intended to give you a chance to reflect on what a consultant should consider from an external/internal perspective when working on an OD/change effort for a client and developing a plan on how to evaluate the success of the effort. After you have scanned internally and externally for information, the next step is feeding back the information as you work with the client to develop a strategy, of course evaluating that plan is high on the "to do" list.

7.4 Context Setting

Organizational change is driven by external events (Austin 2015), and this is why many books, articles, and Internet accounts share stories of organizational failure, which may have led to "an extinction event" or organizational disappearance (Frank et al. 2014).

A key way organizations can proactively address any form of change is by initiating an OD effort, which refers to a long-range effort to improve an organization's problem-solving capabilities and its ability to cope with changes in its external environment with the help of external or internal behavior-scientist consultants, or change agents (French 1982). This definition takes into consideration the holistic, systemic, and comprehensive approach to organizational change. However, sometimes the change need comes from within to address a myriad of issues like morale, change in mission or vision, or even structure.

This holistic and systemic approach reinforces why both external and internal sources and resources need to be considered when developing an evaluation strategy intended to measure the success and impact of organizational change effort. An evaluation strategy is incomplete without considering both external and internal sources. As an organization embarks on a change effort, the leadership team should consider both sources.

Because it is important to plan evaluation from the start, the search for the external and internal sources/resources begins there too. As Stephen Covey once wrote as the second habit in his book *7 Habits of Highly Effective People*, one should consider "to begin with the end in mind" (Covey 1989). Like any project you might embark on, you will need a plan, and as you pursue helping a client with a change effort, you need to plan the evaluation strategy (Phillips & Phillips 2011) with the external and internal sources in mind. This positions the leadership to take a comprehensive and holistic view and approach. An organization does not exist in a vacuum, and for this reason, factors external and internal to the organization need attention so the entire picture comes into focus.

7.5 Evaluation Considerations

There are organizational trends that are causing organizations to change, and this has implications for external and internal factors when developing an OD/change plan along with an evaluation strategy. The following sample trends include some of the changes that organizations have to address and that could serve as a source of external and internal information when developing a change strategy. After each sample trend, a *scan* suggestion will be provided to guide you in this task.

1. A *technological explosion* has occurred around the world. For starters, the amount of technology being used by organizations and its employees is growing at an exponential rate. Today, there are more mobile devices on the planet than there are people (Boren 2014). The increasing use of technology around the world and within organizations means that organizations will need to develop a workforce that can capitalize on the technological changes (Bhargava, 2016).
   a. **Scan**: Look at the company's social media presence and ways they use technology to communicate and get the work done. Look for information that can shed light on the problem, or underlying problems, that they are trying to address. What has been shared in the local, state or national media?
2. *Leadership development* is needed but often shortened or wiped out altogether due to lack of funds. Leaders who positively manage their relationships with their workforce get positive results, yet organizations seem to continue to hire and promote managers with great analytical

skills and poor social skills (Rock 2013). This will need to change going forward in order for organizations to be successful.

   a. ***Scan***: Evaluate the relationships between leadership and staff, between leadership and external vendors/donors/supporters/financiers, and between employees to assess how interactions are going and at what level the leaders are performing. This internal and external data may help the team to understand barriers and challenges to change or fill in parts of the root cause of the problem.

3. There are *demographic* changes occurring in the United States particularly with the growth of traditionally held minority groups. For example, it is estimated that, by 2020, Hispanics will represent 74% of the labor force growth (Llopis 2015). This changing demographic presents organizations with opportunities and challenges for leaders and employees to engage in productive and effective relationships with their community (Rodriguez 2007). This growing demographic is just one of several with the overall minority growth expected to outgrow the present majority population. Diversity is and will continue to be an increasing strategic imperative, challenge, opportunity, and advantage for organizations.

   a. ***Scan***: When gathering information to detect root cause or to supplement the information provided by the organization, the OD consultant should look to the surrounding community. How is the company engaging? Do community members serve in an advisory role? Can they provide guidance on issues that affect the organization (for instance, on environmental issues)? How does the community experience the organization?

4. To add to the previously mentioned diversity, there are presently *four generations* in the workforce, with Millennials and Baby Boomers playing a key role in organizations. Baby Boomers are expected to live longer, work longer, and have a lot of institutional knowledge that requires a human capital strategy in order to share with others before they retire and move on from their respective organization (Hesselbein & Goldsmith 2009). Millennials, on the other hand, are growing and they in turn want freedom, corporate integrity, and openness, and to have fun at work, while being impatient and want things quicker while aspiring for innovation, something that all organizations will need in order to change (Tapscott 2009). This adds an increased need for organizations to adapt to this changing workforce.

   a. ***Scan***: The scan here takes a few different tracks. First, is there a need to look at intergenerational issues within the organization—are there barriers, myths, challenges that need to be addressed? What does the customer base represent? Are there lag issues with Millennials and Generation Y being attracted to the product? For instance, has the company fallen behind on "green initiatives" and does that affect the willingness of certain customers to buy from them or use their services?

Next, what are the recruiting practices polices, and overall culture experiences for the various generations represented now and of those they are looking to hire—do any of them impede recruitment? Retention?

5. Continuing to add to the workforce diversity, there is an *aging workforce*. The world is aging and it is not just the United States (United Nations 2002). It is estimated that, by 2030, the majority of the countries around the world will face a labor shortage owing to the aging workforce (Strack 2014). This will add to the increased urgency for organizations to develop a human capital strategy with the large retirement eligible and aging workforce.

   a. **Scan**: Building on the answers to number 4, what has been done to retain the vast knowledge older workers own before they leave the organization/knowledge transfer is a much-ignored practice. Many retirees and even those just leaving for a new role depart with contacts/networking, historical knowledge, and content knowledge without anyone amassing that golden information before parting ways. From an *internal perspective*, organizations should assess what are the perceptions of this aging workforce through an organizational survey or focus groups.

These are just some of the trends that can be influencing organizations going forward, forcing them to adapt and change. Any of these trends present a challenge and opportunity by itself, but the reality is that for most companies they are occurring simultaneously (Mouriño 2014). All organizations are and will be faced with these trends and changes, some more than others.

The following section highlights both external and internal sources to consider when an organization looks to adapt and change with these trends. This approach provides a holistic information-gathering process that augments the development of the evaluation strategy. The following are some external and internal sources to consider in addressing them when considering an OD/change effort and evaluation strategy.

7.6 Technological Explosion

From an *external perspective*, there should be an assessment and conversations with local or regional educational institutions that provide the development of these skills. Here, you can gain insight into what these institutions see when it comes to registrations and the output of those attaining the needed technological skill sets. In addition, the learning & development department within HR should be speaking with vendors that provide these services to assess partnering opportunities for developing the organization's workforce.

From an *internal perspective*, a conversation with the chief information officer (CIO) of the organization and some of his or her key leadership team as to the future IT strategy is a good place to start. Here, you can gain insights into what is the technological strategy for the organization and in turn what skill set needs to be translated into. This conversation with the CIO and his or her leadership team can lead to an assessment of the skill makeup of the workforce.

The CIO's perspective and insights can then lead to a deeper conversation with the chief human resources officer and some of his or her executive team as to the skill set needed for the organization going forward and as to the workforce strategy needed to address these changes. Here, you can have a conversation regarding any competitors in the industry, globally and locally, and how your organization stacks up against the competition when it comes to this particular area.

Gaining access to the organization's HR analytics point of contact can serve as an invaluable partnering opportunity. Working with this individual or team can help in gaining access to the organizational skill set level and in turn organizational needs going forward. This individual/team should have access to recruitment, retention, attrition, demographics, education and certifications, future potential retiree data, and just an overall comprehensive view of the human capital of the organization.

There should be a discussion with the organization's learning & development department to assess what sort of plans or strategies they have in place or planned in order to address this workforce skill development need. There should also be conversations with the leadership team that focus on the organization's business strategy development. These areas of the organizations will be assessing what markets to go into, markets to get out of, and the skill sets needed for the organization.

Once these conversations have taken place, it can lead to more conversations with key leaders within the organization in assessing the present level of competence in the organization and the level needed to be attained. These leaders can include those from key departments that will be affected earlier on.

7.7 Leadership Development

From an *external perspective*, organizations should consider assessing the latest research on leadership development, which also includes best practices for managing a virtual workforce. This can be done by reviewing research or white papers from organizations such as Gallup, Center for Creative Leadership, Development Dimensions Inc., and the Pew Research Center, along with various colleges and universities, just to name a few. Other professional organizations to consider are Society for Human Resources, Association for Talent & Development, and the Organization Development Network. Last, there are experts in the field of evaluation in many areas including leadership development like Dr. William J. Rothwell and Dr. Jack Phillips who have written extensively on the topic and conduct consulting and certification on evaluation at a global level. In addition, the organization's internal HR department can also benchmark external best practices of other organizations and research leadership competencies needed for the future.

From an *internal perspective*, the organization's HR team should be having conversations with their executive team on the leaders' skill set and competencies needed for organizational success. An assessment of the organization's recognition strategy, tools, and performance management practices used by leaders is an important factor to consider and should be conducted by the HR organization with recommendations for the executive team. Last, conducting an organizational survey of the employee workforce on their perspective on recognition, employee engagement, and the employees' perspective on their leadership may well provide critical insights into the organization.

7.8 Demographics

From an *external perspective*, organizations should consider gaining actual data as to the demographics in the local area where the organization is presently based, whether this is one area or situated around the country. HR should access external professional organizations and associations that encompass different cultures, industries, and special interest groups as appropriate. An external source may be research or print media that helps them to gain an understanding of needs and dovetails with the local input they received in person or through other data-gathering techniques.

From an *internal perspective*, the organization's leadership should partner with their HR department to conduct an analysis of their internal demographics that include future potential retirement population, succession planning, leader competencies, and where the organization presently stands when it comes to this changing demographic. Another assessment that may be helpful is a valuation of the company's diversity and inclusion practices. This assessment could focus on one group, for example the Latino/Hispanic workforce, or include all minorities and women to ensure that the broader demographic changes/needs are being addressed. A partnership between the parent company and minority or specialty resource groups (e.g., disabled veterans) can help with climate, awareness raising, recruitment, and so on.

In summary, while the above trends are real and happening across the globe, they are used here *as an example* to highlight what organizations and their leadership should consider when addressing change, creating an evaluation strategy, and scanning both external and internal sources/resources for information to support plan development or data gathering.

7.9 Chapter Summary

It is probably appropriate to end this chapter where it started. An important means by which organizations can proactively address any form of change is by initiating a long-term strategy to address improvement efforts in an organization. This OD/change improves an organization's problem-solving capabilities and its ability to cope with changes in its external environment with the help of external or internal behavior-scientist consultants, or change agents (French 1982). With this in mind, the following thoughts regarding OD/change (though general and broad) are relevant and hopefully helpful:

- Always approach these types of OD/change issues from a holistic perspective. Keep in mind both other *external and internal sources and resources* that will provide a more complete comprehensive assessment.
- No matter what information the client presents, dig deeper to uncover all the variables/needs. Asking probing questions can facilitate uncovering the root cause of the request.

- An OD consultant is an advisor. The problem belongs to the client, and you serve as a guide, counsel, and researcher.
- The tools, techniques, checklist, and so on are just that. Accessing them at the right time and place will benefit your client. This book's tools are not all-encompassing and should be used as a starting place.
- Go slow to go fast. Review and scan all the possible internal and external sources of information to make sure you have all the data before beginning. In order to decrease the chance of missed opportunities it is wise to feed back the information to the client as well as the team. OD/change issues are not solved overnight. Make clear the goals and objectives—this may take a few attempts.
- Begin with the end in mind. Ensure clarity on what the client is trying to solve and make sure everyone is on the same page. Engagement on all levels is strategic.

In summary, this chapter looked to address both the external and internal factors that an organization, their leadership, and their OD and HR practitioner or consultant should consider when developing an evaluation strategy for their OD/change efforts. The chapter attempted to do this by providing an introduction to the topic and by using as an example a set of current trends that force organizations to adapt and change with external and internal sources/resources to consider. The chapter also presented a case study that focused on a change effort request from a client with external and internal sources to consider. Last, the chapter provided a couple of pragmatic sets of concepts, tools, and template checklists to use when considering both external and external sources when developing an evaluation strategy for an organizational change effort. Hopefully, this chapter has demonstrated the importance of external/internal sources when developing an evaluation strategy for an organizational change effort.

Because this book is about OD/change evaluation, perhaps an acronym will help.

7.10 Tools

Tool 7.1: External and Internal Sources Assessment Tool

The following table and checklists can be used as a template when addressing trends like the ones mentioned here regarding potential external and internal sources to consider. This is a sample for you to add, revise, and delete as needed.

	External and Internal Sources Assessment Tool		
Contacted Explored Date	*External Trends Source*	Contacted Explored Date	*Internal Trends Source*
Technology			
	Educational institutions		Chief Information Officer (CIO)
	IT training vendors		Key managers
	Social media		Human resources (HR)
	Organization-related technology		Analytics (HR, quality, etc.)
			Executive leadership
			Employees
			Social media
Organization-Related Materials			
	Prior change efforts with external sources		Executive team—ensure you understand their perspective on the change effort and their end goal
	Outside vendors experiences—surveys, feedback		Human resources
			Business strategy executive—ensure you gain insight into these individual's perspectives.
			Previous change efforts— what has been done in the past—gather that data. Consider time frame— redo or keep?

(Continued)

External and Internal Sources Assessment Tool			
Contacted Explored Date	*External Trends Source*	*Contacted Explored Date*	*Internal Trends Source*
	External leadership education		Organizational surveys, climate assessments
	Published outgoing material (brochures, videos)		Learning and development—previous internal education programs
	External complaints		Employees' feedback
			Prior complaints
			Dashboard—sales, productivity, financial metrics
Data			
	Local demographic data		Executive leadership
	Professional minority organizations		HR analytics professional—gain valuable information as to the numbers and metrics. This will be part of the business case for any change
	Subject matter experts (consultants)—consider collaborating with an expert in the area you are working on. One example on evaluation is the ROI Institute		Collaborate with professional interest groups
	Professional associations—related to the industry or project being worked on		Key mid-level managers—ensure you understand their perspective and role in the change effort

(*Continued*)

External and Internal Sources Assessment Tool			
Contacted Explored Date	*External Trends Source*	*Contacted Explored Date*	*Internal Trends Source*
	Research firms—entities that conduct research in your particular project. For example, Center for Creative Leadership, Developmental Dimensions Inc., Pew Research, and so on		Employee demographics—education levels, skill sets, competencies, and so on
Special Populations			
	Assess best practices of competitors		Gain insights through surveys, interviews, focus groups: manager, employees, executive leadership
	Benchmarking: compare what other organizations are doing		Is the org engaged in *knowledge transfer* from retiring or ready to leave employees?
	Community demographics—how has the org responded to changing needs?		Unions
	Community activists		Gain insight from the HR department
	Local, state, or federal government officer		
	Business and industry councils		
	Community service providers or other industries		Conduct a survey or focus group with this workforce

These are not intended to be exhaustive lists but to highlight and brainstorm other sources.

Tool 7.2: General External and Internal Sources and Questions to Consider with Your Evaluation Strategy

The following is a higher-level perspective on potential sources to consider when scanning both the external and internal environment when it comes to evaluating the organization's OD/change effort. They include the following:

1. What is driving the organizational change effort?
2. What strategy is the organization pursuing?
3. What is the workforce's skill makeup?
4. Does the skill makeup need to be upgraded?
5. What systems are or need to be in place?
6. What processes are needed or need to be revisited?
7. Is the organization organized in the proper manner to compete?
8. Will the culture support the upcoming changes? If not or not sure, what is needed?
9. Is the organization ready for these changes?
10. If not, what will it take to get the organization ready?
11. Will there be resistance to the change? If so, why?
12. Do people not understand, like the change, or believe who's leading the change? If not, what should you do to address these?
13. How much time do you have to adapt, develop, and change?

These questions form a foundation for a candid dialogue with key leaders and stakeholders within the organization.

References

Austin, J. (2015). Leading effective change: A primer for the HR professional. SHRM Foundation's Effective Practice Guideline Series. Retrieved from: https://shrm.org/about/foundation/products/Documents/8-15%20Leading%20Change%20EPG-Final.pdf

Berinato, S. (2014). A framework for understanding VUCA. Retrieved from: https://hbr.org/2014/09/a-framework-for-understanding-vuca/

Bhargava, M. (2016). *The Internet of things and mindset V1*. Retrieved from: https://www.linkedin.com/pulse/internet-things-mindset-v1-siddharth-bhargava

Boren, Z. D. (2014). There are officially more mobile devices than people in the world. Retrieved from: http://www.independent.co.uk/life-style/gadgets-and-tech/news/there-are-officially-more-mobile-devices-than-people-in-the-world-9780518.html

Covey, S. (1989). *The Seven Habits of Highly Effective People.* New York: Fireside.

Frank, M., Roehrig, P., & Pring, B. (2014). *Code Halos: How the Digital Lives of People, Things, and Organizations Are Changing the Rules of Business.* New Jersey: Wiley.

French, W. (1982). *Organization Development Principals and Practices.* As cited in: Cummings T. G., & Worley, C. G., *Organization Development & Change,* 2015, 10th edition. Stamford, CT: Cengage Learning.

Hesselbein, F., & Goldsmith, M. (2009). *The Organization of the Future 2.* San Francisco, CA: Jossey-Bass.

Koivisto, J., Vataja, K., & Seppanen-Jarvela, R. (2008). Relational evaluation of organizational development activities. *International Journal of Public Administration, 31*(10–11): 1167–1181.

Kotter, J. P. (2007). Leading change: Why transformation efforts fail. *Harvard Business Review,* January, 2007.

Llopis, G. (2015). Without Hispanics, America's corporations can't grow and compete. *Forbes Magazine.* Retrieved from: http://www.forbes.com/sites/glennllopis/2015/03/17/without-hispanics-americas-corporations-cant-grow-and-compete/

Maurer, R. (2010). *Beyond the Wall of Resistance.* Austin, TX: Bard Press.

Mouriño, E. (2014). *The Perfect Human Capital Storm: Workplace Challenges & Opportunities in the 21st Century.* North Charleston, SC: CreateSpace Independent Publishing Platform.

Phillips, P., & Phillips, J. (2011). *The Consultant's Scorecard: Tracking ROI and Bottom-line Impact of Consulting Projects.* 2nd edition. New York: McGraw-Hill.

Rock, D. (2013). Why organizations fail. *Fortune Magazine.* Retrieved from: http://fortune.com/2013/10/23/why-organizations-fail/

Rodriguez, R. (2007). *Latino Talent: Effective Strategies to Recruit, Retain and Develop Hispanic Professionals.* New Jersey: Wiley.

Strack, R. (2014). The workforce crisis of 2030 and how to start solving it now. Retrieved from: http://www.ted.com/talks/rainer_strack_the_surprising_workforce_crisis_of_2030_and_how_to_start_solving_it_now#t-721653

Tapscott, D. (2009). *Grown Up Digital: How the Net Generation Is Changing Your World.* New York: McGraw-Hill.

United Nations. (2002). World population ageing: 1950–2050. Population Division, DESA, United Nations. Retrieved from: http://www.un.org/esa/population/publications/worldageing19502050/

Chapter 8

Determining, Collecting, and Analyzing Implementation Data

Robert Boswell

Contents

8.1 Introduction

At the heart of evaluating an organization's intervention efforts is a reliance on determining, collecting, and analyzing data. Cummings and Worley (2008) posited "evaluation is concerned with providing feedback to practitioners and organization members about the progress and impact of interventions." Hence, a thorough evaluation is really the only way the organization stakeholders can be certain whether the change effort has been effective or not. Furthermore, evaluation data provide essential contributions to decision makers on determining whether to continue, modify, or discontinue a change initiative.

8.2 Chapter Overview

Data, data, data, these are at the top of every solution list. We point to the data for answers and look to obtain more data, but are the right data being shared, do they measure what we need them to, and are they being analyzed correctly? All important questions for an evaluation plan. In this chapter, we focus on several critical issues associated with

1. Determining types of data to collect
2. Data collection methods
3. Analyzing implementation data

8.3 Business Case: Evaluating a Leadership Development Program

Between November 2001 and March 2002, a national college association conducted a summit to determine how best to develop and sustain leaders. The aim of this effort was to address the looming leadership shortage in community colleges. There were different constituent groups involved consisting of experts in community college leadership from the affiliate councils, college and state "grow-your-own" programs, colleges in underserved areas, and university programs (American Association of Community Colleges 2003). As a result, many community colleges across the nation begin putting in place leadership development programs including a college along the

East Coast. In this case, the OD intervention is the implementation of the Leadership Institute (LI).

The major goal of the LI is to develop leaders within the community college by fostering the ability of individuals to meet the challenges faced by the college in an era of rapid change. It was during the 2001–2002 academic year that the LI at a local community college was first established. At one point, the LI was being implemented every academic year, but because of budget constraints, it now runs every other academic year. The target population includes faculty, administrators, and classified/confidential staff who are interested in seeking leadership positions in the future or honing their skills for the positions they currently hold. There have been 153 participants over a 12-year span. Participants meet in 10 sessions over the course of the academic years (45.25 hours). Academic Affairs covers the cost of the LI, which is approximately $8500 each year (does not include facilitators' time). The selection process includes an application that consists of essays, recommendations, signatures of commitment, and resume. A committee reviews and ranks the applications using established criteria.

Case Study Questions

Refer to the content in this chapter to answer the following questions pertaining to the above case study.

1. What *during* application-appraisal data may be useful in ascertaining that the LI was implemented as intended?
2. What *after* application-appraisal data may help determine if the LI was a success or not?
3. Based on the Balanced Scorecard (BSC) approach, which of the four areas (financial stewardship, customers/stakeholders, internal business processes, and organizational capacity) does the LI align with the most? Explain.
4. Which two data collection methods would best measure the effectiveness of the LI implementation? Explain.
5. You are tasked with determining the type of data to collect and the analysis methods. In this case, what would be your top three choices? Remember to consider both qualitative (typically begins as non-numerical, open-ended) and quantitative (typically numerical) choices.

8.4 Determining Types of Evaluation Data

Determining types of data to collect focuses on selecting variables and designing reliable measures of those variables. So, how does an organization determine what types of data to collect when evaluating OD interventions? It is not unusual for most discourse and practices of evaluation to relegate evaluation to after an intervention has been implemented. However, it has been disputed that the after application understanding of evaluation is only partly accurate. That is because the after application understanding assumes that the intervention has been implemented as prescribed and the significance of evaluation is to measure their outcomes. However, most interventions are not implemented as prescribed (Trader-Leigh 2002). There are many explanations for the inadequate implementation of an OD intervention, including workplace politics (Pfeffer 1982), strong socialization and cultural norms (Neumann 1989), insufficient information, poor timing and lack of necessary resources (Kotter & Schlesinger 1979), and poorly planned implementation of the change initiative (Winum et al. 1997). The succeeding sections will look at various types of data collection options as well as analysis methods.

Earlier in Chapter 6, criteria for the evaluation process were discussed and, if done at the start of the process, set the foundation for the guidance in this chapter. On the basis of the bigger plan, the data needed should become clear.

8.4.1 Appraisal

Evaluation can examine a few aspects of a change effort: the change effort itself or the solutions the change effort is trying to address. Evaluation aimed at assessing how well the change initiative is being implemented may be called during application-appraisal. Evaluation intended to ascertain whether the change initiative is producing the expected outcomes may be called after application-appraisal. During application-appraisal is usually concerned with intervention variables and after application-appraisal is usually concerned with outcome variables. In determining the data to collect for evaluating an OD intervention, these two types of evaluation inform the process and collecting both types is necessary in many cases.

During application-appraisal data are collected frequently at shorter intervals. Measures may consist of underlying features of the change intervention, perceptions of the individuals involved, and information regarding the immediate effects of the intervention. Examples of measures may involve productivity associated with the implementation of a new technology, user satisfaction with the new technology, and organizational commitment to implement the new technology. These data provide information about how the change initiative is progressing.

After application-appraisal takes a lengthier amount of time to gather and interpret. It would include all the data from during application-appraisal as well as additional outcomes, such as absenteeism, turnover, maintenance cost, quality, and productivity. These data provide feedback that might indicate that the OD intervention is producing expected results or not and should be sustained or terminated.

8.5 BSC Application

Besides considering evaluation in terms of during application-appraisal and after application-appraisal, it also is essential to consider evaluation of OD interventions derived from the organization's goals. That is, an organization is only effective to the degree by which they meet their goals. One useful tool to assess change initiatives is the BSC developed by Robert Kaplan and David Norton (1996). In determining what types of data to collect, Kaplan and Norton argued that besides the traditional financial data, we also need to consider three other very important types of data when evaluating OD interventions: customer data, internal business process data, and learning/growth data. Kaplan and Norton (1996) suggest specific measures for each of the four types of data. The following identifies the data collected and some generic measures for each:

■ Financial—return on investment, cash flow, financial results
■ Customer—satisfaction, retention, customer returns
■ Internal—quality assurance, process alignment, bottlenecks
■ Learning and growth—employee job satisfaction, training, development

These data may be used to align business activities to an organization's strategic objectives. However, it is paramount to know the mission statement and strategic plan of the organization first and foremost. Once the strategic plan is understood, the four perspectives generally outlined in the BSC approach serve as areas that may be considered for improvement when evaluating OD interventions.

These areas are not comprehensive and are often organization specific. Therefore, it would be necessary for each organization to analyze the specific and quantifiable results in each of the four areas as they relate to their organization. Each of the four perspectives is mutually dependent, but improvement in one area will not necessarily lead to improvement in other areas. Utilizing the BSC approach to evaluate organization change initiatives may assist a company in meeting their strategic objectives. Nonetheless, ongoing feedback is critical and should be contributed to by everyone within the organization.

In the planning meetings, the four areas can be examined and more specific criteria can be defined. This process helps make a strong connection between the change effort goals, evaluation criteria, data needed, and analysis methods. On the basis of the goals of the effort, the team should ask the following questions:

A. What are we trying to achieve? Do our goals reflect the final desired outcomes? (If no, rewrite)
B. What measurement criteria will help us define these goals?
C. What data (types of data) do we need to collect to understand whether or not we have met the goals?
D. What is the best method for analyzing the data? What method will give our stakeholders the most accurate information?

Let us try an example by looking back as the business case.

A. Goal: Develop leaders within the community college by fostering the ability of individuals to meet the challenges faced by the college in an era of rapid change.

   Analysis: Seems a little confusing—here is a rewrite: *Develop leaders with adaptability and flexibility who use those skills to meet the needs of a college setting.* Adaptability, flexibility, and other metrics, under their control, within the college can be measured.
B. Measurement Criteria: Here are some options:
   a. Improvement in fiscally sound responses to change
   b. Actions taken in response to accreditation changes
   c. Staff morale, sense of security, collaboration, in times of change
C. Types of Data: Adaptability and flexibility can be measured in a few ways, here are some options:
   a. Interviews with the main participant, their coworkers, or subordinates
   b. Review of prior situations

      c. Self-assessment through survey

      d. Financial data

      e. Admissions

      f. Employee retention

D. Analysis Methods: This answer depends on specifically what you are trying to show. If you need to demonstrate better financial outcomes, then projections can be helpful. If the goal is to show improved flexibility, then a more complicated analysis will look at multiple variables that might evidence better accreditation scores or higher applications or improved employee satisfaction scores. The data can be displayed visually and on paper—Chapter 9 speaks to how to report out the findings and shares ideas for how to best tackle this task.

8.6 Collecting Data

The data collection methods discussed in this chapter include interviews, observations, questionnaires, and unobtrusive measures. These are some of the foremost techniques for collecting data to evaluate OD interventions. Additionally, there are other data collection techniques suitable to OD evaluations such as focus groups, nominal group technique (problem identification, solution generation, and decision making), and work samples (observing employees doing activities). However, there is no single data collection method that can fully measure the variables important to OD. Each data collection method has certain strengths and weaknesses. Table 8.1 lists some of the pros and cons for each method discussed in this chapter. When evaluating an OD intervention, it is often best to utilize more than one data collection method as well as multiple sources of data, which is known as data triangulation (Denzin & Lincoln 1994). That is, when multiple data sources and methods converge; more credibility is generated than if the evaluation had been limited to one source or method.

8.6.1 Interviews

Interviews are possibly the most extensively used technique for data collection in OD. They can be conducted in person, by phone, or by computer technology such as Skype, Adobe Connect, or Google Hangouts. The human interaction that occurs during interviews is perhaps the chief benefit of interviews. Interviews typically fall into three simple types: structured, semistructured,

Table 8.1 Data Collection Methods: Pros and Cons

Methods	Description	Pros	Cons
Interviews	Structured, semistructured, or unstructured one-on-one discussions with key members within an organization	• Ability to tailor line of discussion • More personalized • Opportunity to explore issues in depth	• Expensive • Time-consuming • Produces limited quantitative data • May be difficult to analyze and summarize findings • Small sample size
Observations	The process of observing organizational performance in natural or controlled settings	• Does not rely on self-reports • Generates relevant, quantitative data • Setting may be natural, flexible, and unstructured	• Contamination • Expensive • Time-consuming • Halo effect • Observer bias • Small sample
Questionnaires	Standardized paper-and-pencil or web-based surveys that ask predetermined questions	• Ability to reach large groups • Easy to administer • Inexpensive • Easily generates quantitative data	• Impersonal • Limited opportunities to explore issues in depth • May have low response rates
Unobtrusive measures	Archival or extant data already collected by an organization in their records or archives	• Low cost • Usually highly accurate • Easy to compare or identify trends	• May be difficult to access data • May not provide a complete picture of the situation • Often out of date

and unstructured interviews. A structured interview is very similar to a questionnaire where individuals choose from responses already provided. For example, in assessing employee attitudes toward a new technology being implemented organization-wide, the interviewer may ask, "How important is it to you to see the new technology successfully implemented? Is it critical, very important, important, or not important? Structured interviews are often used in telephone interviews, which, for some purposes, can provide data similar to those acquired through face-to-face interviews at a lower cost.

Semistructured interviews do not have prearranged responses. Instead, the questions are open-ended but specific in intent, enabling individual responses. For instance, an interviewer may ask, "What are some things you really like best about the new technology?" The question is objective, but it allows for probing, follow-up, and clarification. It is the most common type of interview for evaluating change initiatives in organizations.

Unstructured interviews are open-ended and wide-ranging. The interviewer has an overall goal and asks questions pertinent to this goal. Consequently, there is some leeway in what is asked, and often somewhat different questions are used with each interviewee. The unstructured interview could be challenging to conduct. It is highly subjective and requires substantial expertise. Irrespective of the type of interview, it is vital that the questions are worded so that the individual is not led to a specific answer. The interview questions should be tested with a small group before they are used with the official participants. The pilot test can ask the sample to describe what they think the question is asking and compare it to what is the intended focus. Another good check is to practice interviewing to make sure that the interviewer is approachable, easy to talk to, and willing to share clarifications. Interviews offer a wonderful opportunity to make a connection and gather information not likely amassed by filling out a survey.

8.6.2 Observations

The observation data collection method involves the process of collecting data by witnessing organizational performance in its natural settings. This may be done by walking informally through a work area scanning the environment and its participants or by counting the frequencies of particular kinds of behaviors. Observing should be done with as little intrusion as possible. Of course, once a new person enters the situation, he or she changes it just because of his or her presence. Observation can take a few interactions in order to allow everyone to go back to their "typical behaviors" so that a more natural encounter occurs. All participants should be informed of any data collection in advance; applicable state and federal laws will apply, for example, the number of times a receptionist used (or avoided) the new system to schedule appointments for patients.

Observations may vary from complete participant observations to more detached observations. Participant observation is when the observer becomes a member of the group or situation being observed. Detached observation is when the observer is not part of the group or situation being observed. When observations are correctly used, they afford discerning data about an organization's intervention success.

8.6.3 Questionnaires (Survey)

The questionnaire (survey) is also a commonly used type of data collection in evaluating OD change efforts. It is composed of written text statements or questions used to gain participant perceptions, attitudes, beliefs, values, perspectives, and other qualities. Questionnaires are used widely because of the efficiency they provide in obtaining data about an eclectic range of change efforts, from surveys of massive populations to reactions of employees to different management methods. Questionnaires can be utilized to measure a variety of traits and can take numerous formats. Some of these formats may comprise Likert-type scales, checklist, or ranked items. This type of tool can be done online and data can be pulled into a database, which makes it very efficient, and it may necessitate additional information technology resources to create the online format and the database but will save lots of time in the end and lend itself to slick data visualization options.

A questionnaire/survey typically gathers mostly ranked responses; however, there is another type of question, the open-ended one that can be added. The open-ended question can really enhance the depth of responses on any of the topics in the ranked questions or on a new topic altogether. Questions that ask for a ranking or yes/no cannot fully ascertain all the variables on a topic and the open-ended one allows participants to share the rest of their thoughts. A tool that gathers qualitative and quantitative data often provides a better portrayal of the criteria being evaluated.

8.6.4 Quantitative Data/Unobtrusive Measures

These types of data refer to extant data or secondary data often already collected and available such as absenteeism or tardiness rate, turnover rate, productivity, or financial performance. Unobtrusive measures are useful in evaluating change effort outputs at the organization, group, and individual levels. They serve as a valuable complement to other evaluation data collection methods, such as interviews and questionnaires.

Many organizations and their boards respond well to numbers data that easily display progress to goals. In some instances, the data that are needed may not be currently collected. This should be addressed during planning meeting and actions should be identified if the data exist or if a data collection tool needs to be devised. The team will need to consult with data analytics, information technology, quality, or other experts in the organization to ask questions and work out a plan. It may be important to include some of these players on the team as well.

8.7 Analyzing Implementation Data

Analyzing implementation data comprises two comprehensive approaches: qualitative and quantitative. Qualitative analysis is usually considered a "bottom-up" or an inductive approach that is open to new ways of understanding. The aim is to generate conception regarding the OD intervention being evaluated. Quantitative analysis is considered a "top-down" or a deductive approach where predetermined understanding limits the analysis of evaluation data. That is because evaluators formulate assumptions according to an already developed model or concept and then gather data to prove or disprove them. Although quantitative analysis has become the established mainstream methodology, the use of both approaches provides a more accurate analysis for evaluating OD interventions.

8.7.1 Qualitative Analysis

Data analysis of qualitative data includes preparing and organizing the data for analysis, narrowing the data into themes through coding, and finally representing the data (Creswell 2012). This approach is commonly used to analyze data collected via documentation reviews, focus groups, or interviews. There are several qualitative analytic techniques. According to Maxwell (2012), these techniques may fall into three key groups: (1) memos, (2) categorizing strategies (such as coding and thematic analysis), and (3) connecting strategies (such as narrative analysis).

For OD evaluation, we will focus on categorizing strategies, which is a more common technique for analyzing interview data. Categorizing analysis can summarize interview comments into a few themes that capture new insights from participants about the issues related to an OD intervention. The foremost categorizing strategy in qualitative analysis is coding. The coding process involves gathering the text into lesser categories of information. These lesser categories of information are commonly called themes. Themes in qualitative analysis are comprehensive units of information that comprise several codes combined to form a shared idea. Once this process is complete, evaluators move to interpret and represent the data.

Interpretation involves extracting outside of the codes and themes to the developed implication of the data. It is a progression that begins with recognizing codes, constructing themes after the codes, and then the organization of themes into larger units of generalization to make sense of the data. Representing the data comprises packaging of what was found in the text, tabular, or figure form (Creswell 2012).

8.7.2 Quantitative Analysis

Quantitative analysis is commonly used to analyze data collected via observations, questionnaires, or secondary data. Analyzing quantitative data involves a wide range of methods from simple descriptive statistics of a measure to the more sophisticated structure equation modeling (SEM). The most common methods for analyzing quantitative data associated with OD interventions are means, standard deviations, correlation coefficients, and scatter grams. Computing a mean and standard deviation for each item on a questionnaire provides the participants' average score and variability, which may offer the most cost-effective and direct way to summarize quantitative data.

Correlation coefficients and scatter grams allow OD consultants to make inferences regarding the relationships between variables. The strength of a relationship between two or more variables may be illustrated. If an organization has implemented a new system to address a claim processing problem, a correlation coefficient may be useful. To determine institutionalization

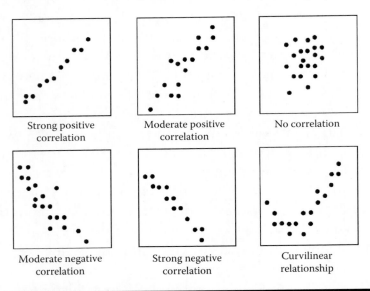

| Strong positive correlation | Moderate positive correlation | No correlation |
| Moderate negative correlation | Strong negative correlation | Curvilinear relationship |

Figure 8.1 Basic scatter plot patterns.

of the new system, the OD consultant may examine the relationship between variables readiness to change and self-efficacy.

A scatter gram is an illustration of the relationship between two variables. Six simple patterns can materialize from a scatter gram, as shown in Figure 8.1. For the sake of simplicity, it will briefly describe three: positive correlation, negative correlation, and no correlation. The positive correlation shows that as one variable increases, the other increases. The negative correlation shows that as one variable increases, the other decreases. Finally, when there is no correlation, there is no pattern to the points, indicating no connection between the two variables.

8.8 Chapter Summary

The key issues associated with determining types of data to collect, data collection methods, and analyzing implementation data were discussed in this chapter. Evaluation was discussed in regard to two essential views: *during application-appraisal*, with a focus on whether the change initiative is being implemented as intended, and *after application-appraisal*, focused on whether the change initiative is generating the projected results. These two kinds of data aid in determining implementation data to collect.

A BSC approach was explored as a means to determining implementation data to collect. In determining what types of data to collect, Kaplan and Norton (1996) argued that besides the traditional financial data, we also need to consider three other very important types of data when evaluating OD interventions: customer data, internal business process data, and learning/growth data. This approach involves giving much consideration to an organization's goals and strategy.

Evaluation of OD interventions also involves decisions about data collection methods and sources of data. The data collection methods we discussed in this chapter included interviews, observations, questionnaires, and unobtrusive measures. The pros and cons of each method were reviewed.

Analyzing implementation data is composed of two comprehensive approaches: qualitative and quantitative. Data analysis of qualitative data includes preparing and organizing the data for analysis, narrowing the data into themes through coding, and finally representing the data. This approach is commonly used to analyze data collected via documentation reviews, focus groups, or interviews. Quantitative analysis is commonly used to analyze data collected via observations, questionnaires, or secondary data.

Analyzing quantitative data involves a wide range of methods from simple descriptive statistics of a measure to the more sophisticated structure equation modeling. The most common methods for analyzing quantitative data associated with OD interventions are means and standard deviations.

8.9 Key Definitions

After application-appraisal: Assessments intended to discover after intervention outcomes, such as performance, job satisfaction, productivity, and turnover.

Coding: The process of merging the text or visual data into small classifications of information, seeking confirmation for the code from different databases being used, and then assigning a label to the code (Creswell 2012).

Data analysis: A process of reviewing, cleaning, converting, and displaying data with the goal of ascertaining useful information, suggesting conclusions, and supporting decision making.

During application-appraisal: Assessments aimed at guiding organization development during implementation of intervention.

Focus group: A form of data collection in which perceptions, opinions, beliefs, and attitudes were elicited from a group of people toward a particular service, concept, product, packaging, or idea.

Interviews: A conversation between two or more people where questions are asked by the interviewer to elicit facts or statements from the interviewee.

Nominal group technique (NGT): A technique used for group problem-solving technique where each member is asked to generate a list of ideas without communicating with their colleagues.

Observations: The methods of observing people directly while they are performing their duties or assigned activities.

Qualitative analysis: A process that involves organizing the data for review such as interview transcripts, observation notes, or unobtrusive measures in order to describe, classify, and interpret the data.

Quantitative analysis: An analysis of data gathered by means of complex mathematical and statistical modeling.

Questionnaires: A research instrument consisting of a series of questions and other prompts for the purpose of gathering information from participants.

Themes: Broad units of information that consist of several codes collected to form a shared idea.

Triangulation: The convergence of various data collection methods and sources to interpret outcomes.

Unobtrusive measures: Data indirectly collected from participants that are from secondary sources such as records and archives in the organization.

Work sample: A collection of samples of work the individual or group has done to showcase skills.

8.10 Activities for OD Practitioners

Activity 8.1: Conduct a 30-Minute Interview, Record, and Transcribe It

1. Conduct a 30-minute interview assessing the strategies utilized to implement an OD intervention using the *Interview Guide for Evaluating OD Implementation Strategies* found in the tools section of this chapter. Record and transcribe the interview.

Activity 8.2: Code Interview Transcript

2. Analyzing the interview transcript from Activity 8.1 by coding or merging the text into smaller classifications of data and assigning a label to each classification.

Activity 8.3: Administer Process of Change Questionnaire

3. Adapt the *Organization Development Processes of Change Questionnaire* found in the tools section of this chapter to a change effort taking place at an organization you have access to, and then report the means and standard deviations.

8.11 Tools

Tool 8.1: Interview Guide for Evaluating OD Implementation Strategies

10 Questions for Evaluating OD Implementation Strategies
1. Is the change effort being communicated in the organization? If so, how?
2. How do you feel about the change effort and how do you communicate those feelings in your organization?
3. How could or do you help others realize the positive impact of the change effort at your organization?
4. How could or do you consider your organization's identity, desires, and success can be enhanced by the change effort?
5. How could or do you empower individuals to participate the change effort at your organization?
6. Explain your level of commitment to implementing the change effort at your organization.
7. What cues or reminders have been added by your organization for the implementation the change effort?
8. What new activities or thought processes has been substituted for old activities and thought processes concerning the change effort?
9. Does your organization reward individuals for participating in the change effort? If so, how?
10. What social support or help is available with taking the steps for implementing the change effort at your organization?

Source: Adapted from Boswell, R. A. (2011). A physician group's movement toward electronic health records: A case study using the transtheoretical model for organizational change. *Consulting Psychology Journal: Practice and Research, 63*(2), 138–148.

Tool 8.2: Organization Development Processes of Change Questionnaire

Instructions: The following experiences can affect organizational change behaviors of some people. Think of any similar experiences you may be currently having or have had *in the last month.* Then rate the *frequency* of this event on the following 5-point scale.

There are five possible responses to each of the items in the questionnaire:

1 = Never
2 = Seldom
3 = Occasionally
4 = Often
5 = Repeatedly

Please read each statement and circle the number on the *right* to indicate how often each event occurs. Remember that these statements refer to situations you may have had *during the past month*.

	Never	Seldom	Occasionally	Often	Repeatedly
1. I can expect to be rewarded if I participate in the change effort.	1	2	3	4	5
2. I have someone I can count on when I'm having problems with the change effort.	1	2	3	4	5
3. I react emotionally to the need to have the change effort succeed.	1	2	3	4	5
4. I see the change effort impacts all involved in a positive way.	1	2	3	4	5
5. I get correspondence about the change effort (e-mail, meetings, newsletters, etc.).	1	2	3	4	5
6. Old ways of working have been substituted with new ways of working.	1	2	3	4	5

(Continued)

	Never	*Seldom*	*Occasionally*	*Often*	*Repeatedly*
7. I find our organization changing in ways that makes it easier to participate in the change effort.	1	2	3	4	5
8. I feel more competent when I participate in the change effort.	1	2	3	4	5
9. The information from trainings about the change effort helps.	1	2	3	4	5
10. We keep things around at the workplace that remind us of the change effort.	1	2	3	4	5
11. I have someone who listens when I need help with the change effort.	1	2	3	4	5
12. Stories about the change effort failing upset me.	1	2	3	4	5
13. I become disappointed with myself when I depend on the status quo.	1	2	3	4	5
14. I consider the view that the status quo can be detrimental to the organization.	1	2	3	4	5
15. I will be more effective in my position because of the change effort.	1	2	3	4	5

(Continued)

	Never	Seldom	Occasionally	Often	Repeatedly
16. The organization generally replaced anything associated with the status quo.	1	2	3	4	5
17. I find that participating in the change effort is a good substitute for the status quo.	1	2	3	4	5
18. The organization rewards me for implementing the change effort.	1	2	3	4	5
19. I am 100% committed to the change effort.	1	2	3	4	5
20. I notice that we have been moving toward the change effort for a while.	1	2	3	4	5

Source: Adapted from Prochaska, J. O., Velicer, W. F., DiClemente, C. C., & Fava, J. L. (1988). Measuring the process of change: Applications to the cessation of smoking. *Journal of Consulting and Clinical Psychology, 56,* 520–528.

References

American Association of Community Colleges. (2003). *Leading forward: Growing your own leadership development programs.* Retrieved from http://www.aacc .nche.edu/newsevents/Events/leadershipsuite/Pages/developmentaspx

Boswell, R. A. (2011). A physician group's movement toward electronic health records: A case study using the transtheoretical model for organizational change. *Consulting Psychology Journal: Practice and Research, 63*(2), 138–148. doi:10.1037/a0024319

Creswell, J. W. (2012). *Qualitative Inquiry and Research Design: Choosing among Five Approaches,* 3rd ed. Thousand Oaks, CA: Sage.

Cummings, T. G., & Worley, C. G. (2008). *Organization Development & Change,* 9th ed. Mason, OH: South Western Cengage Learning.

Denzin, N. K., & Lincoln, Y. S. (Eds.) (1994). *Handbook of Qualitative Research.* Thousand Oaks, CA: Sage.

Kaplan, R. S., & Norton, D. P. (1996). *The Balanced Scorecard: Translating Strategy into Action*. Boston, MA: Harvard Business School Press.

Kotter, J. P., & Schlesinger, L. A. (1979). Choosing strategies for change. *Harvard Business Review, 57*(2), 106–114.

Maxwell, J. A. (2012). *Qualitative Research Design: An Interactive Approach*, 3rd ed. Thousand Oaks, CA: Sage Publications.

Neumann, J. E. (1989). Why people don't participate in organizational change. In Woodman, R. W., & Passmore, W. A. (Eds.), *Research in Organizational Change and Development*, pp. 181–212. Greenwich, CT: JAI Press.

Pfeffer, J. (1982). *Power in Organizations*. Boston, MA: Pittman.

Prochaska, J. O., Velicer, W. F., DiClemente, C. C., & Fava, J. L. (1988). Measuring the process of change: Applications to the cessation of smoking. *Journal of Consulting and Clinical Psychology, 56*, 520–528.

Trader-Leigh, K. (2002). Case study: Identifying resistance in managing change. *Journal of Organizational Change Management, 15*, 138–155.

Winum, P., Ryterband, E., & Stephenson, P. (1997). Helping organizations change: A model for guiding consultation. *Consulting Psychology Journal: Practice and Research, 49*, 6–16.

Chapter 9

Reporting Results to Stakeholders

Maureen Connelly Jones

Contents

9.1 Introduction

The importance of stakeholders has been discussed in multiple chapters and here again the role of that group will be highlighted. Reporting results is frequently relegated to the final phase along with evaluation. However, if the report of results plan is crafted well, it can facilitate additional change and highlight a well-executed blueprint that energizes the employee base and stakeholders alike. "Evaluation reports may be the only lasting record of a program or project, including the results achieved and lessons that were learned from its implementation" (Oxfam GB, n.d.). Getting the right information in the right hands helps your stakeholders support your organization and any effort to improve your bottom line. Benefits of a reporting relationship include allowing the change effort team to gather more feedback, invigorate the team, and close the loop on project phases or interventions.

9.2 Chapter Overview

This chapter will provide a guide for reporting results to your various stakeholders. Challenges and ideas for how and when to get the information on the desks of your key players will be addressed. The procedure for selection of stakeholders was addressed in Chapter 5. This section will also explore the best methods for disseminating the information as well as ideas for tracking what can be a complex communication procedure. This chapter is about follow through—the project goals, the inclusion of stakeholders, and the transparency needed for all involved to continue to stand behind an important change effort.

9.3 Business Case

A 10-month change effort to improve the fundraising efforts of a medium-sized not-for-profit has come to a close. The organization began their effort because donors were slowly pulling out and management was hearing rumblings of dissatisfaction with customer relations but no formal complaints were lodged and they could not discern what caused the downturn. They hired an organization development (OD) consulting group to help them sort through the issues and make a plan to get back on track. After one-on-one as well as focus group sessions, it was becoming clearer that employees were not comfortable with the way donations were being solicited, which resulted in strained relationships with donors and an avoidance to embarking on new connections.

A company-wide survey that looked deeply into how employees (including leadership) felt about their connection to the mission, transparency issues, and trust was distributed. The survey had some Likert-type scale questions as well as an equal amount of open-ended opportunities that gave them a place to share their impressions and feelings. The OD team, in their initial information gathering stage, found that most of the employees have been with the company since its inception and felt a deep tie to its core values. It was this detail that triggered an early-than-expected feedback meeting with the CEO. He was concerned but glad this had come to light and gave the team the go ahead to dig deeper and help them construct viable solutions. One caveat, though, he did not want to involve any donors or outside vendors in the change effort or feedback. The OD consultants spent some time educating him on the benefits of external stakeholders but he felt it was too risky.

The project plan was created, including the evaluation plan. The CEO and the OD team disagreed on how often and to whom the evaluation feedback should be reported—he was fine with sharing details with the executive team but wanted to wait until the end to bring in the employees and external stakeholders. Again, the OD consultants provided evidence-based education and then continued on with his plan.

Multiple interventions were delivered and all were received well. A new data collection tool was created by the vice president of donor relations that provided employees with a script to improve engagement with their donors. The executive team felt like this would decrease the negativity that the potential donors might have been feeling.

Along the way, employees were very curious about the data that were gathered and how else they could help. Some information was shared, after checking with the CEO, but most was directly shared only with the chief operating officer, finance director, and donor relations. Data collected at the halfway point showed little to no improvements. At this point, the OD team had the analysis of the open-ended data and scheduled a meeting with the CEO. They pulled together the multiple data points and proposed a few additional opportunities to communicate the process, some findings, and then open up to questions and idea sharing. A discussion about the donor script was had and the lack of improvement in incoming donations was revealed. No conversations or information gathering were done with this group.

Case Questions

1. How do you think the decision to keep the stakeholders out of the data gathering and feedback loop affected the overall process?
2. How could the employees have been a service to the process?
3. What do you think might have been the CEO's reasons for limiting communication to the executive group?
4. What could the OD consulting team have done to move the CEO's decisions about information sharing?
5. What stakeholders should the CEO have included in the process? Why would you have included them—what are the benefits?
6. Little improvement was realized at the halfway mark, what do you think was the cause?
7. How would you have crafted the communication plan during the change event?
8. If you could have convinced the CEO to include the employees and outside stakeholders, how would you have changed the final communication of results?

9.4 Critical Role of Reporting

Reporting should be invigorating, challenging, and also serve specific goals, like the rest of the change effort. Sharing results is the culminating event in an often long and challenging process even if it has been a positive experience. Mid-project, final, or a customized report can create a positive impact on an organization, employee group, or community, which is a powerful prospect. Development of a strong evaluation process that includes avenues for reporting results prevents a common problem: results being forgotten and missed communication opportunities. Evaluation findings can be used to improve a program, generate new knowledge, support enhancements, build new shared meaning and understanding, show program effectiveness, improve community services, communicate an investment in shared goals, and so many other positive outcomes (Kellogg, 2004, pp. 110–112).

Obstacles, some known and some that will make a surprise showing, must be deliberately discussed. What will stand in the way of using the evaluation results and how can they be avoided or minimized? Obstacles may include the following: results being different from expected, fear of being judged (Kellogg, 2004), resistance to change, poor organization functioning, and a poorly run process. Any of these can cause tension for leaders. Effective reporting is one way to assure thorough, clear, and consistent communication of project results.

9.4.1 Effective Reporting

Creating and presenting reports is not just reproducing the same information gleamed from the change effort. It is so much more, it is about performing, which I suggest is a method to share a story or information to an audience that makes an impact. The communicators in this presentation will need to ask themselves a few questions as they prepare each report. Target audience identification, language, length, style, scope, translation needs, format, and stakeholder needs are among the important elements to define.

Who is the target audience? Identifying how many audiences and what they are looking for in each evaluation report will help tailor messaging, language, length, and style. For example, if the project is improvement in productivity, you have two audiences—staff and financial backers—each may get the same information but language, length, and style may vary. Avoid surprising folks at the end by keeping them in the loop throughout the project, which may require education for the leadership team to understand the rationale for this technical.

9.4.2 Scope of the Report

After the target audience(s) is clear, decisions about scope need to be answered. Each audience, which may include just one person, will often necessitate their own slight modifications. Just because the evaluation results in many details, it does not mean that a detailed report is the best way to proceed (Holm-Hansen, 2008). The following are questions that will help determine scope:

■ How much does this audience need to hear at this time? Reporting results can occur at intervals during the project and at the end, and for follow-up.

- Can each audience get the same base information with small customized details?
- Is there any information that cannot be shared and whom does that affect?

9.5 Communication Strategy

Crafting a strategy for communicating results should, once again, be completed at the start of the project and be revised as needed along the way. The strategy should include a decision about who will be the communicator, does the organization have someone with the right skills on staff, defining communication channels, blueprint for a dissemination plan, and then crafting the plan itself. Selecting the right one will be an important role in the project. An overarching goal should be to help the audience(s) understand the data by keeping it in lay terms and clear enough to draw connections between results and action steps.

9.5.1 Communication and Dissemination Plan

Who will be the communicator? This role requires another special skill set. Whomever is chosen should be selected because they can easily translate complex information, is easy to talk with, and is approachable when asked for clarification. A leader can ascertain this evaluation by asking internal customers as well as outside vendors or clients for suggestions. After the face of the project is selected, the plan development takes front and center.

9.5.2 Determining Stakeholder Groups

Part of the plan will include determining stakeholder groupings. It is likely that different types of information should be shared with different constituents and possibly at different intervals. For example, the board may want weekly briefings about sales numbers and outside donors may need only monthly reports that may also include overall donations and restricted fund information. One option is to create groupings of stakeholders that all have the same information and communication needs. Organize the type and

frequency of the data sharing. Determining what information is dissemi-
nated to whom is an early key task.

9.5.3 *Identifying Communication Channels*

Another significant task is to investigate what communication channels are
preferred by each group. It is important to listen carefully in meetings with
stakeholders and the executive team members as they share how best to
share the information and with whom. Listen to stakeholders in regard to
what they really need and what information will be of benefit. Of course,
there will be time for direction questions during planning meetings. Next,
ideas for developing the report will be discussed in more detail.

9.6 Developing the Report

The next mission will be to develop the report particulars including organization of the report elements, context and background, timing, plans for
translating the data, and presentation formats. The following are questions to
help guide the report preparation:

- With whom are we sharing these data?
- What data need to be shared?
- What data are most helpful to each stakeholder/group? Do we know of
  any special needs?
- What format is best to share the data?
- How often do the data need to be presented?
- Where will the data be presented (if live)?
- Who will present the data to each stakeholder/group?

Call out key findings. Make it easy to read and understand. Start with the
"must know" first to value the reader's time. Highlight important points with
boxes, changes in font size, bold or italic type (Kellogg, 2004) so that the
reader/audience is drawn to what you think is important. Translation is so
critical to engaging all the stakeholders. The report needs to be easily under-
standable, have a good flow, and encourage readability. What is the reading
level? Make sure that it is inclusive of all readers. Contemplate alternate ways

to share the information that increases share-ability and usability like creating an infographic.

9.6.1 Timing

A decision on timing will be dependent on a few factors such as audience, intent, availability of data, and stakeholder needs. Reporting of results can be an energizing time for all involved as the steps toward progress are shared. This is a time to reveal good news—progress toward goals. It is also an opportunity to set directions and tell audiences what will happen next as well as what revisions to the plan have been made and why. Timing of reports might be weekly, monthly, quarterly, or a final report. Timing may also be anchored with the specifics of the fiscal year, important associated projects, or seasons. Work out the details and revisit to maintain control over the sources and programming of your results.

9.6.2 Types of Reports

What do the executives, employees, and key stakeholders need to know more about? This can guide the type of report that is chosen and can be adjusted based on the phases of the project or the outcomes being evaluated. Beginning with what you hoped the audience takes away can make the choice clear. Here are some examples of report types for your consideration:

- **Summative:** programs or projects are assessed at the end of an operating cycle, and findings are typically used to help decide whether a program should be adopted, continued, or modified for improvement (Austin Independent School District, n.d.).
- **Formative:** programs or projects are typically assessed during their development or early implementation to provide information about how best to revise and modify for improvement. This type of evaluation is often helpful for pilot projects and new programs, but it can be used for progress monitoring of ongoing programs (Austin Independent School District, n.d.).
- **Action-oriented:** a clear connection between the results and an action plan based on recommendations is made in this type of report.
- **Storytelling:** this format uses a story that exemplifies the change effort so that the audience can connect with the results.

- **Evaluation snapshot:** a short summary that includes key details.
- **Case study:** a study of a person, groups, organization, often qualitative in order to gather a more in-depth understanding of the issues.
- **Newspaper/website/media:** articles or columns can be written about the findings or key players can be interviewed.
- **Executive report/summary:** typically one page, providing a summary of the findings. Just the facts. May include appendices with additional information.
- **Lessons learned:** this approach speaks to what was learned from the change effort process, interventions, and findings but is used to help others learn from one organization's experience.
- **Impact reporting:** report using charts, which can be easier to interpret and can save high-level executives' time.
- **Question and answer:** this option would typically be used in addition to one of the other formats. Organizations do not always allow question-and-answer sessions and if they are not open to it, that should be communicated in advance of any format. However, it can help clarify and energize others about the findings.

Next steps—what will you do with the results—how will it make an impact, address specific stakeholder information gets bundled in one or more types of reports depending on the audience, purpose, and organization needs? This list includes just some of the possible format choices, as has been shared in previous chapters, and should be customized to the effort.

9.6.3 Context and Background

Again, depending on the audience, the report should describe the context and background of the change effort (share as much as wanted or is necessary). This should include the stated problem that prompted the process. Help set the context for why this effort was started and why resources were allocated to the planning and implementation. This step also allows for a comparison between the situation at the start and hopefully the improvement that will be reported at the moment or at the final reporting.

9.6.4 Language

The language used in the reports can either pull the reader in or push them away. If the language is too complex or full of jargon, the reader may not take the time to digest the information, which takes away the benefit of reporting altogether. If the words used are difficult to understand, maybe too academic or industry specific, the reader will feel lost and again less likely to read and then participate in the rest of the effort. The following are questions to ask when you are deciding what language feel you need:

- Are the acronyms, jargon, or industry-specific words being used hard to understand for someone not in the field?
- Does the language fit the target audience?
- Does the language engage the audience member?
- Do any of the necessary terms or concepts need to be defined in the report?

9.6.5 *Customization Decisions*

Each stakeholder is interested in specific key pieces of information beyond the main findings, recommendation, and action plan steps. One option to address those precise needs is to customize reports based on conversations with stakeholders that identified what information benefits them most. For example, shareholders may not be interested in the new employee satisfaction results (although they might if pre-education is completed and they understand the impact of engaged employees on the financial status) so their report may provide general change effort results and then recommendation and action plan particulars that affect the financial landscape. These conclusions will be tailored to the organization, stakeholder group, and project, so plan for time to discuss the plan and be flexible if it appears customization is needed.

Caution with customizing as it is time consuming and unintentionally may leave out vital information. Tailoring a report can be efficient and give a concierge-type feel but it does take additional resources and planning. Cassidy (2015) suggests that reporting tools be aligned in order to tell one story and avoid the possibility of diluting your message.

Key performance indicators (KPIs): Best practice reporting using the KPIs identified in your evaluation plan. Assure that the KPIs are defined so that the reader can be clear on the interpretation of better/worse over time. Benchmark each KPI alongside the target metric as they are reported.

9.7 Data Visualization

Data are not meaningful by themselves; they need to be reviewed and analyzed for meaning (Oxfam GB, n.d., p. 4). Data also need to be connected to decisions (outcomes and goals). Data are powerful, and evaluation reports should capitalize on this power to communicate results and change. Each intervention and result has a visualization method that suits its features best and should be carefully planned. The OD consultant or whomever is in charge of choosing how the data are displayed needs to have competencies in data analytics and statistics to assure that the correct method is chosen and reveals accurate results. For example, be sure that the chart chosen is suited for the data you display. For example, pie charts explore one variable and bar charts look at the relationship between two variables (Machtmes, 2011). Options for presenting the data are plentiful. This section will speak to a few of those options and some cautionary suggestions.

Charts and graphs can be an eloquent approach to sharing the hard work and outcomes of any project, especially a change event. Each selection should include a title with clearly labeled and defined variables. Do not assume the reader will understand how to decipher the visual, the data points, or the interpretation. Colorful and easy-to-read charts, graphs, and tables can enhance the interest and long-term comprehension of a well-planned evaluation/change effort. It will require someone to translate the findings into easy-to-digest segments. A graphic display goes a long way in accomplishing this objective. Here are some examples of tools:

- Bar graph: Used when comparing various items or ideas.
- Histogram: Used to show frequency and compare items or ideas; each bar represents an interval of values.
- Line graph: Used to show change over time.
- Pictograph: Used to show frequency and compare items or ideas.
- Circle graph (or pie graph): Used to show parts or percentages of a whole.
- Box-and-whisker plot: Used to show the range of values as well as the median, quartiles, and outliers; five-number summary is another name for this representation.
- Line plot: Used to easily organize one group of data.
- Scatterplot (or scattergram): Used to determine if a correlation exists between two data sets, and how strong it is, also used to calculate line or curve of best fit.

■ Stem-and-leaf plot: Used to show frequency; data are grouped according to place value, using the digit in the greatest place (Teacher Vision, 2017).

Consistency will help those less familiar with data analytics to monitor progress. It may be advisable to report out in the same manner each time if you choose a long-term reporting strategy. Decreases confusion and allows the reader to learn the method one time and feel comfortable with subsequent versions. Provide a key that explains all of the elements to avoid confusion and to decrease instances of misinterpretation.

Here are some additional resources for displaying data:

■ The Lynda.com library of videos including how to create charts and graphs. This site has extensive videos on how to use Microsoft Excel, which is a very helpful tool when organizing and displaying data
  – https://www.lynda.com/ and https://www.lynda.com/search?q=charts
■ Using graphs or charts to illustrate quantitative data:
  – www.cdc.gov/healthyyouth/evaluation/pdf/brief12.pdf
■ Using graphics to report evaluation results:
  – http://learningstore.uwex.edu/Using-Graphics-to-Report-Evaluation
    -Results-P1022.aspx
■ How can I make a pie chart in excel to report data?
  – http://www.extension.psu.edu/evaluation/pdf/TS64.pdf

9.7.1 Live Dashboards

Another exciting option is to use a live dashboard tool. Live dashboards will provide real-time data that stakeholders can check on at any time (Cassidy, 2015). They can be project generic or be tailored to the stakeholder or group. Because this unique option sidesteps the analysis phase, it should be used alongside other analyses (Cassidy, 2015). This endeavor will require support from graphics and information technology but can serve the project as well as internal request for project metrics. Regular updates will require resources to input new data and can keep the interest in a project and enthusiasm for the work high. Both are a challenge when projects are long term, have participation challenges, and when they are so big it is tough to see smaller incremental changes. Designing in a way that is easy to interpret is critical; if it is too hard to interpret, it will be a wasted resource.

Of course, each dashboard element should be connected to the already defined metrics and a clear link to the goals should be evident.

Take advantage of tools that support this work. Spreadsheet tools make it easy to collect, analyze, and display data. There are companies that can do this for you for a fee. Other options include free software or software packages already licensed by the organization. If resources are an issue, then turn to your networks to see if you can use talent or resources to accomplish this goal. Translating can be a time-consuming undertaking, but the benefits are great. Clearly displayed data are easy to understand, which adds to the ease at which the results can be used and then shared.

9.8 Engaging Stakeholders

Engagement makes a difference and that holds true for reporting the results of an evaluation. Because evaluation can be complex, it is vitally important to translate the information into something useable by all those involved. The stakeholder group may change at any point in the change effort, so be open and aware of new partners who join the organization or new external partners. Watching for new opportunities to expand the network can avoid missed opportunities.

Another stakeholder consideration is that of mergers and acquisitions. With the changing landscape of federal regulations, tightening financial resources, increasing insurance premiums, and changing consumer practices has come a litany of mergers and acquisitions. This creates unfamiliar environments for many organizations where there are new leaders and new processes. Some of these circumstances necessitate change efforts that become even more complex to coordinate.

A final consideration for this section is to create a space for stakeholders to feed information back to the planning team. This will need to be communicated clearly to stakeholder groups. A communication avenue after the report will provide an opportunity to feed back usefulness and future needs. Some of these reactions can be beneficial in the feedback loop and revision processes that are uniquely an OD event.

9.8.1 Pre-Education

Each stakeholder comes to the change effort with various experiences in the organization, industry, or situation. Assuming that each stakeholder has the requisite knowledge to understand the process and provide feedback would be a mistake. One way to avoid making them feel out of sync or just unknowledgeable is to assess each one for specific educational needs before and during the change effort. This can be as simple as a quick conversation at a meeting or more involved interview that assesses current and future needs. Knowledge is power, and in this instance, engaging stakeholders can show commitment to their involvement and to a well-crafted project.

9.9 Evaluating the Reporting Process

Evaluation occurs at all phases of the change project and evaluating the evaluation is no different. Seeking feedback after each report of findings will give planners insight into how it was received, understood, and interpreted. Feedback can be obtained through a quick online or written survey. There are free online survey options that make this an efficient way to collect comments. Groups to consider include any stakeholder who received reports or attended briefings. Suggestions for survey items are as follows:

- Did you understand the information shared? If not, why not?
- You can ask specific questions about the results and/or ask for a break-down comparison of results to original change event purpose and goals.
- Were the displays of data (graphs and charts) easy to understand? If not, why not?
- In your opinion, what information was missed?
- Was there too much, just enough, or too little information? Explain.
- Please share how you experienced the format of the report—likes, dislikes?
- Were there any key players missed?

Gathering real-time feedback allows the project to stay nimble and responsive to its stakeholders and project sponsor(s). Changes can be made right away to improve the next report.

9.10 Chapter Summary

There are numerous reasons why a report will or will not be used by the organization, its employees, and stakeholders. Sometimes, it is hard to understand or know all the influences that affect the usability of the report.

This chapter has outlined best practices for developing and delivering findings but that still may not be enough. Political context or climate could rocket findings to the front page of the paper or get it buried (SAMHSA, 2016). A quality evaluation increases the validity and in turn the ability for interested parties to share and generalize the findings for use in other projects or situations. Another consideration is the availability of technological support to disseminate the information and make it available. Getting it on websites or updating live results options takes resources that may not have been available or allocated in the master plan. Finally, the results may go against other reported findings and cause some tension. This is more reason to make sure the program evaluation is solidly grounded in good methodology and adheres to strict metric assessment standards. The goal is to develop a rigorous evaluation plan and report of findings that have been crafted with precision and attention to detail whatever the results may be.

Asking questions early and understanding the internal and external culture and climate can help make strategic decisions to downplay the impact of these forces.

9.11 Key Definition

Data visualization: the presentation of data in a pictorial or graphical format. It enables decision makers to see analytics presented visually, so they can grasp difficult concepts or identify new patterns (SAS Institute, 2016).

9.12 Tools

Tool 9.1: Stakeholder Communication Tracker

Rationale: Reporting the final results is an important task but communicating results throughout the process is even more important and can reap many benefits: continued enthusiasm, revitalization if the momentum is slowing, keeping key players in the loop to maintain engagement, and transparency.

Directions:

■ Decide who is accountable for completing this tool—if this responsibility lies with one person or multiple people and communicate.
■ This tool is best suited for an Excel spreadsheet and then is easily sharable.

- Column 1: Populate with all the stakeholders/stakeholder groups.
- Column 2: Note their role within the organization or group name and role.
- Column 3: If they have been assigned to a specialty group (a smaller group of stakeholders that are focused on a particular phase or element of the project). Note all groups they may belong to (some may be connected to a few areas).
- Column 4: Note who in the organization or consultant is responsible for communicating with each stakeholder.
- Column 5: Note each time communication had been made with the stakeholder/group.

Stakeholder	Role or Organization	Group Assignment	Person Accountable	Communication Contact Dates				

Tool 9.2: Checklist for Reporting

Rationale: Checklists are very helpful in keeping the project on track. Communicating out results can be complex, and this tool could be created in a project management software option. Project Libre is free software that would benefit any project tracking.

Directions: Fill in each column with the necessary information to track the report creation. This tool can organize all the reports, or if they are customized, then there may be a need for one tool per customized report.

Report Creation Checklist			
Topic	Person Accountable	Timeline	Resources Needed
Communication strategy plan created			
Communicator(s) chosen			
Identification of report goal			
Audience identification			
Audience pre-education			
Engagement of stakeholders			
Timing			
Context and background			
Format type			
Customization needs			
Jargon and language critique			
Data visualization choice			

Tool 9.3: Evaluation Reporting Organizer

Rationale: This tool can help organize the reporting requirements across the organization and to external stakeholders. This tool format can be used in spreadsheet format and shared as needed—likely an easier format to keep up to date.

Directions:

- Row one includes the topic headings
- Row two includes questions to be asked that can determine the details needed for each column

Stakeholder or Group Name	Data Needed	Timing	Format	Who Will Communicate Results?	Resources
Who is the audience? Preferred contact method	What do they need to know? Specific result elements, financial data	How often do they need to get results? Weekly, monthly, quarterly, final only	Executive summary In-person website, dashboard update	Name	Printing, media, rental, additional experts to implement, travel

References

Austin Independent School District. (n.d.). What is the difference between formative and summative evaluations? Retrieved from: https://www.austinisd.org/dre/ask-the-evaluator/whats-difference-between-formative-and-summative-evaluations

Cassidy, K. (2015). How to engage business stakeholders with analytics data. Building blocks. Retrieved from: http://blog.building-blocks.com/insights/how-to-engage-business-stakeholders-with-analytics-data

Holm-Hansen, C. (2008). Communicating evaluation results: Tips for conducting program evaluation. Wilder Research. Retrieved from: https://www.wilder.org/Wilder-Research/Publications/Studies/Program%20Evaluation%20and%20Research%20Tips/Communicating%20Evaluation%20Results%20-%20Tips%20for%20Conducting%20Program%20Evaluation%20Issue%2014,%20Fact%20Sheet.pdf

Kellogg, W. K. (2004). W.K. Kellogg Foundation Evaluation handbook. Retrieved from: https://www.wkkf.org/resource-directory/resource/2010/w-k-kellogg-foundation-evaluation-handbook

Machtmes, K. (2011). How to present program evaluation data to stakeholders using charts. Retrieved from: https://lsuagcenterode.wordpress.com/2011/06/03/how-to-present-program-evaluation-data-to-stakeholders-using-charts/

Oxfam GB. (n.d.). Oxfam GB evaluation guidelines. Retrieved from: http://www.alnap.org/resource/10016.aspx

SAMHSA. (2016). Reporting your evaluation results. Retrieved from: http://www.samhsa.gov/capt/tools-learning-resources/reporting-evaluation-results

SAS Institute. (2016). Data visualization: What it is and why it matters. Retrieved from: http://www.sas.com/en_us/insights/big-data/data-visualization.html

Teacher Vision. (2017). Displaying data. Retrieved from: https://www.teachervision.com/graph-chart-0/displaying-data

Chapter 10

The Future of Evaluation in Organization Development

William J. Rothwell

Contents

10.1 Introduction

It never ceases to amaze me that trainers and managers seem to be obsessed with return on investment and other forms of evaluation for training, but few people ask for rigorous evaluations of long-term, organization-wide change efforts like organization development (OD). For every one publication on OD evaluation (for instance, see Golembiewski 2002), dozens of books and articles have been published on training evaluation (see Kirkpatrick & Kirkpatrick 2006; Phillips & Phillips 2012). Why is that? Training is a short-term change effort focused on individuals; OD is a long-term change effort focused on groups of people or on entire organizations. Which one is more important, costly, time-consuming, and difficult? It just seems that too much focus is placed on justifying the cost of training while too little focus is placed on assessing the impact of organizational change. That is especially true because a high percentage of organizational change efforts fail to achieve desired results or match management expectations.

In this final chapter of the book, I would like to offer some predictions about the future of evaluation in OD and invite readers to make their own predictions, plan for addressing the trends, and build competencies essential to evaluating OD interventions.

10.2 Nine Predictions about Evaluating OD

Let me take out my crystal ball, gaze into it, and offer nine predictions about evaluation in OD. In the future...

1. OD interventions will be more often evaluated.
2. OD practitioners will become more skilled in facilitating a process by which members of the organization develop measurable change objectives.
3. OD interventions will be tracked by individuals, teams/groups, departments/divisions, and organizations.
4. OD will be measured by change impact tied to the organization's balanced scorecard, on one hand, and to individual key performance indicators (KPIs), on the other hand.

5. OD evaluations will be flexible to accommodate for changing conditions.
6. OD evaluations will be technology enabled, using virtual surveys, focus groups, interviews, and dashboards.
7. OD evaluations will move away from an exclusive focus on "what's wrong" and will include "what's right."
8. OD evaluations will move away from an obsession with quantitative methods and will include qualitative methods, making for true "mixed methods" evaluations.
9. OD evaluation will increasingly be linked to assessment and diagnosis so that the reasons for the change effort are closely related to the results secured from the change efforts.

10.2.1 Trend 1: OD Interventions Will Be More Often Evaluated

The trend is for all human-oriented programs to be an increased focus of evaluative efforts. It just makes sense to conclude, then, that OD interventions will be more often evaluated. All management efforts are under scrutiny to ensure that money is well spent and that unnecessary costs can be reduced.

10.2.2 Trend 2: OD Practitioners Will Become More Skilled in Facilitating a Process by Which Members of the Organization Develop Measurable Change Objectives

Traditionally, many OD practitioners have come from a background of psychology or organizational behavior. Psychologists are not known especially for evaluating group or individual therapeutic efforts, and that problems carry over when they facilitate organizational change efforts. Still, as a direct consequence of trend 1, it seems likely that OD practitioners will become more skilled in facilitating how to develop change objectives.

Trainers are accustomed to developing instructional objectives to be achieved upon completion of training. In recent years, they have been encouraged to focus attention on performance objectives by which individuals are measured on how well they apply on their jobs what they learned in training.

In the same way, good OD interventions have measurable change objectives established during action planning. OD consultants should not set the targets. Instead, they should facilitate stakeholders to set their own targets/objectives for OD interventions/change objectives.

Performance objectives and change objectives are based on the same logic: set the measurable targets before embarking on efforts to achieve those targets. But OD consultants do not set the targets; rather, they facilitate the process by which key stakeholder groups set change targets at the organizational, division/department, team, and individual level. It is important to have those change objectives, even though they may have to be modified over time as OD interventions are implemented in a dynamic competitive environment.

10.2.3 Trend 3: OD Interventions Will Be Tracked by Individuals, Teams/Groups, Departments/Divisions, and Organizations

If trend 2 is correct and OD interventions will more often have change objectives established during action planning, then those objectives will provide a basis for monitoring those objectives over long-term implementation. OD consultants will facilitate regular follow-up sessions during implementation to explore answers to such questions as these:

■ Were the objectives complete and realistic?
■ How well are the objectives being implemented at the individual, team/group, department/division, and organizational levels?
■ Why are objectives not being met, and what can be done about problems that arise during implementation?
■ Should objectives be changed or modified as a result of changes in the external environmental conditions faced during long-term implementation?

10.2.4 Trend 4: OD Will Be Measured by Change Impact Tied to the Organization's Balanced Scorecard and to Individual KPIs

Many organizations today establish their organizational strategic goals by using the balanced scorecard (Kaplan & Norton 1996). The logic of the balanced scorecard is that organizational success depends on more than mere financial success, such as profitability, alone. Other issues must also be considered if an organization is to achieve long-term strategic success.

The classic balanced scorecard components are (1) financial, (2) customer, (3) business operations, and (4) organizational learning and growth. The financial sector examines how well the organization establishes, tracks, and achieves its financial goals. The customer sector examines how well the organization seeks to achieve customer satisfaction and grow market share. The business operations sector examines how well the organization efficiently and effectively uses resources to source and deliver products or services. Finally, the learning and growth sector examines how well the organization establishes and maintains an effective corporate culture to support human resources.

Since each organizational unit and individual should support strategic goals, the logic is that some results from departments or individuals are more important than others. They are KPIs, and the KPIs of each organizational unit and individual should be logically related to the scorecard (Keyte 2014).

The same logic can apply to OD interventions. Whenever an OD intervention's change objectives are planned, they should be tied to the organization's balanced scorecard strategic goals. Those, in turn, should be tied to organizational unit and individual KPIs.

The prediction is that, in the future, OD practitioners will get better at helping organizational stakeholders to link their OD intervention change objectives to the organization's balanced scorecard goals and to group/individual KPIs.

10.2.5 Trend 5: OD Evaluations Will Be Flexible to Accommodate for Changing Conditions

It takes time to implement a long-term OD intervention. While some simple interventions can be implemented quickly, many require much time to be successfully implemented. Competitive conditions outside the organization change during long-term change implementation. At the same time, the people in the organization may also change during a long-term change implementation. Consequently, OD evaluations will be flexible and thus subject to modification to accommodate changing conditions.

10.2.6 Trend 6: OD Evaluations Will Be Technology Enabled

Technology offers many opportunities to collect information, feed it back to stakeholders, reach agreement on desired changes, and monitor implementation. In the future, OD evaluations will rely more heavily on technology-enabled approaches. As just one example, many organizations today use dashboards to track progress against change objectives. A *dashboard* is a visual representation of how well an organization, group/team, or an individual is achieving its goals. Many software programs exist on the market to establish and maintain dashboards, which make it easy to display evaluative progress in achieving predefined goals (see, for instance, http://www .softwareadvice.com/bi/dashboard-comparison/). Other websites provide examples of how to set up and use dashboards (see, for instance, http:// dashboardspy.com/).

10.2.7 Trend 7: OD Evaluations Will Move Away from an Exclusive Focus on "What's Wrong" and Will Include "What's Right"

Traditionally, OD evaluation is associated with finding gaps between desired change targets and actual results. The difference between *what should be* and *what is* can be discouraging for some and can lead to efforts to place blame for failures to achieve desired results. (I call these efforts to place blame by the term *blamestorming*.) For that reason, the word *evaluation* can have pejorative connotations.

While it is important to track differences between results and intentions, that may not be enough or may not even be a fair representation of the results. Often it is just as helpful to capture information about what went right during the implementation of an OD intervention. For that reason, OD consultants may rely on storytelling—a key part of appreciative inquiry— and pose questions like these to stakeholders during the implementation of an OD intervention:

> Tell me a story about what made you most proud of your organization during the implementation of an OD change effort:

- What happened?
- When did this happen?
- What did you do, and what results did you get from what you did?
- What was it about the situation that made you feel so proud?

10.2.8 Trend 8: OD Evaluations Will Move Away from an Obsession with Quantitative Methods and Will Include Qualitative Methods

Numbers are important. The current trend toward Big Data and toward measuring HR efforts make them more so. However, when decision makers and stakeholders are presented with quantitative information, they often ask "why is that so?" and "how can that be?" Questions centered around why and how are often best answered by qualitative data. For that reason, OD evaluations will move away from numbers only to include mixed methods that include both numbers and words.

10.2.9 Trend 9: OD Evaluation Will Increasingly Be Linked to Assessment and Diagnosis

Recall that, in the traditional Action Research Model, assessment and diagnosis come early in the change process to surface problems and reach agreement on their importance among decision makers and stakeholders; it is clear that there is a relationship between assessment and diagnosis at the outset of a change process and evaluation as a continuing effort to track how well change implementation is working against agreed-upon change objectives. In the future, this relationship will be more obvious and apparent.

10.3 Making Your Own Predictions

Spend a moment to ponder your own predictions for the future of evaluation in OD. What do you think the trends in OD evaluation are? What makes you think they are trends? What should you and your organization do to address those trends now and as they unfold in the future? What competencies will you, and other OD practitioners, need to address these trends?

10.4 Planning to Address Trends and Build Essential Competencies

As a parting word, I would offer this: It is not enough to identify future trends. OD practitioners in the future must be able to facilitate efforts to plan for their organizations to address these trends and build their own competencies to help their organization address the trends. Refer to the worksheet appearing in Table 10.1 to help structure your thoughts in doing that.

Table 10.1 A Worksheet to Address Trends in OD Evaluation

Directions: Use this worksheet to organize your thinking on OD evaluation trends, what to do about them, and what competencies need to address these trends. For each trend appearing in the left column below, describe in the center column what to do about them and in the right column what competencies OD practitioners will need to address them. Add paper if necessary.		
Trends	*What Should Be Done about the Trends?*	*What Competencies Should OD Practitioners Possess and Use to Address the Trends?*
1 OD interventions will be more often evaluated		
2 OD practitioners will become more skilled in facilitating a process by which members of the organization develop measurable change objectives		
3 OD interventions will be tracked by individuals, teams/ groups, departments/ divisions, and organizations		
4 OD will be measured by change impact tied to the organization's Balanced Scorecard, on one hand, and to individual Key Performance Indicators (KPIs), on the other hand		
5 OD evaluations will be flexible to accommodate for changing conditions		
6 OD evaluations will be technology-enabled, using virtual surveys, focus groups, interviews, and dashboards		
7 OD evaluations will move away from an exclusive focus on "what's wrong" and will include "what's right"		

(Continued)

Table 10.1 (Continued)   A Worksheet to Address Trends in OD Evaluation

	Directions: Use this worksheet to organize your thinking on OD evaluation trends, what to do about them, and what competencies need to address these trends. For each trend appearing in the left column below, describe in the center column what to do about them and in the right column what competencies OD practitioners will need to address them. Add paper if necessary.		
Trends		*What Should Be Done about the Trends?*	*What Competencies Should OD Practitioners Possess and Use to Address the Trends?*
8	OD evaluations will move away from an obsession with quantitative methods and will include qualitative methods, making for true "mixed methods" evaluations		
9	OD evaluation will increasingly be linked to assessment and diagnosis so that the reasons for the change effort are closely related to the results secured from the change efforts		
10	Other trends? (*List them and describe them*)		

References

Golembiewski, R. (2002). *Ironies in Organization Development: Revised and Expanded.* 2nd ed. Abingdon, UK: Routledge.

Kaplan, R., & Norton, D. (1996). *The Balanced Scorecard: Translating Strategy into Action.* Cambridge, MA: Harvard Business Review Press.

Keyte, C. (2014). *Developing Meaningful Key Performance Indicators.* Winchester, UK: Intrafocus.

Kirkpatrick, D., & Kirkpatrick, J. (2006). *Evaluating Training Programs: The Four Levels.* 3rd ed. San Francisco: Berrett-Koehler.

Phillips, P., & Phillips, J. (2012). *Measuring ROI in Learning & Development.* Alexandria, VA: Association for Talent Development.

Appendix A: Stakeholders and the Phases of Change Evaluation

Stakeholder Evaluation Mapping			
Instructions: Determine the goal for the change effort, choose the target(s) of the change effort, and use the actions within each phase of the change process to clarify the influence of the target(s) and create appropriate responses.			
Stated goal of the change effort _____			
Target: Who and When?	*Phase 1: Preintervention*	*Phase 2: Intraintervention*	*Phase 3: Postintervention*
Leadership	• Determine baseline—current scenario • Set clear targets, purpose, criteria, and outcomes for evaluation • Assess alignment of resources for evaluation plan	• Monitor continued commitment and communication of change efforts • Celebrate subgoals achieved • Ensure resources are supplied and if new resources are required	• Assess performance outcomes • Monitor changes in the culture • Determine needs for new intervention; this stage can be a starting point for OD diagnosis

(Continued)

Target: Who and When?	Phase 1: Preintervention	Phase 2: Intraintervention	Phase 3: Postintervention
Participants	• Conduct pretest using multiple data collection methods • Conduct surveys or interviews to determine obstacles including resistance to change	• Progress reports—Continue to evaluate using hard data collection • Interviews—Collect soft data such as confidence in change and resistance to change	• Conduct posttest using same data collection previously used • Observations • Interviews—Collect soft data such as confidence in change and resistance to change
Relevant stakeholder(s)	• Collect baseline satisfaction and performance measures • Questionnaire, interviews (individual and focus group)	• Monitor the internal and external environment for perception and feedback that might affect the ongoing intervention	• Collect postintervention satisfaction and performance measures • Questionnaire, interviews (individual and focus group)

A.1 Key Definitions

Leadership: Those that identify a goal for the organization and sponsor a change effort to achieve this goal.

Participants: Those directly involved in the change effort process. This may include employees at one or more levels and other stakeholders that are critical to the implementation of the change effort.

Relevant stakeholder(s): One or more stakeholders are affected by the change effort. This may include employees other than those directly involved as participants, shareholders, customers, suppliers, and the community.

Appendix B: Change Effort Criteria Evaluation

In this appendix, we have stressed the importance of using independent criteria for evaluation in order to demonstrate the causality of an intervention and, therefore, the internal validity. **Independent** criteria are those for which the results can only be explained by the intervention. **Nonindependent** criteria are those that are potentially explained by factors other than the change effort and, thereby, increase the complexity of evaluation.

The following list of criterion measures might be useful in a preintervention assessment and postintervention evaluation to understand the various influences on the intervention results and to avoid a lack of internal validity.

Directions: Review each criterion in the list below to determine if it is an *independent* criterion or one that must be viewed as *nonindependent*. To complete this part, it may be useful to recall the chapter example using turnover intention. Spaces are available for criterion to be added and considered as applicable to an organization. If needed, offer suggestions for improving the evaluative criteria in the list.

Criterion	Independent	Nonindependent	Improvement
1. Productivity increase			
2. Work engagement improvement			
3. Profitability increase			
4. Turnover reduction			

(Continued)

Criterion	Independent	Nonindependent	Improvement
5. Increase collaboration			
6. Process improvement			
7. Job satisfaction increase			
8. Communication improvement			
9. Cross-cultural literacy improvement			
10. Customer complaint reduction			
11. Transfer of training increase			
12. Waste reduction			
13. Increase readiness for change			
14. Improved customer satisfaction			
15. Reduction in lawsuits			
16. Other:			
17. Other:			
18. Other:			
19. Other:			
20. Other:			

For each criterion in the list:

■ Consider what factors, other than the change effort intervention, might have an influence on the change in each criterion between preintervention evaluation and postintervention evaluation.
■ What further recommendations can be made to improve the measurement of the criterion and the ability to recognize any nonintervention influence?

Index

Page numbers followed by f and t indicate figures and tables, respectively.